HOW TO FIGHT
ANTI-SEMITISM

HOW TO FIGHT ANTI-SEMITISM

BARI WEISS

 CROWN
NEW YORK

All rights reserved.
Published in the United States by Crown, an imprint of
Random House, a division of Penguin Random House LLC,
New York.
crownpublishing.com

CROWN and the Crown colophon are registered trademarks of
Penguin Random House LLC.

Library of Congress Cataloging-in-Publication Data

Names: Weiss, Bari, author.
Title: How to fight anti-Semitism / Bari Weiss.
Description: New York: Crown, 2019. | Includes bibliographical
    references.
Identifiers: LCCN 2019026904 (print) |
    LCCN 2019026905 (ebook) |
    ISBN 9780593136058 (hardcover) |
    ISBN 9780593136065 (ebook)
Subjects: LCSH: Antisemitism—History—21st century. |
    Antisemitism—Political aspects.
Classification: LCC DS145 .W46 2019 (print) |
    LCC DS145 (ebook) | DDC 305.892/4—dc23
LC record available at lccn.loc.gov/2019026904
LC ebook record available at lccn.loc.gov/2019026905

Printed in the United States of America

9 8 7 6 5 4 3 2 1

First Edition

For my grandparents

Andy Weiss, who has always welcomed the stranger.

And Jack Weiss, Kyle Steiner, and Sandy Steiner,
whose memories are for a blessing.

"Proclaim Liberty throughout all the land unto all the inhabitants thereof."

—LEVITICUS 25:10. AND THE LIBERTY BELL.

CONTENTS

HOW TO FIGHT
ANTI-SEMITISM

CHAPTER 1

WAKING UP

There is a shooter at tree of life."

The first text came through our family chat at 10:22 A.M. It was from my baby sister, Suzy. I typed back immediately: "Is dad."

My mouth turned to cotton as I waited for a response to my incomplete question.

My parents live a mile and a half from the Tree of Life synagogue. Three congregations meet in the building for Shabbat morning services; my dad is sometimes at one of them.

"We're home," my mom wrote. "do t worry."

Casey, my second-youngest sister, had heard more: "Magazine high powered ak 47. Doug is on police radio," she said of her husband, a local firefighter.

Someone sent around a link to the Psalms—"in you our ancestors trusted; they trusted and you saved them"—sacred poems Jews have always recited in times of distress. Several texts suggested that there were hostages, early and hopeful speculation. My mom wrote simply: "I'm sure we will know people there."

Minutes slouched by. I turned on CNN. Nothing yet. I refreshed and refreshed and refreshed Twitter every few seconds. There were posts from some local sources urging people to stay away from the area; warnings that the police had shut down that part of the neighborhood; speculation that the shooter might be on the loose. I thought about the Boston Marathon bombers—how one of the Tsarnaev brothers hid in a boat in someone's backyard—and told my parents not to leave the house.

Soon I started getting WhatsApp messages from close friends in Israel, where Shabbat was ending—a strange reversal from the years of the Second Intifada when I would write them: Are you safe?

I checked the news again. Early reports of a shooting in the Squirrel Hill neighborhood of Pittsburgh. No name yet. No victim count. Refresh Twitter.

At some point in those creeping minutes, between Suzy's first text and the moment I booked a plane ticket back to my hometown to witness what the killer had done, my third-youngest sister, Molly, told us that she had heard something on the police scanner.

"He's screaming all these Jews need to die."

. . .

I didn't yet know that I would come to see that phrase as the one that marked the before and the after. That I would come to see that command—the one that had been uttered in a different tongue by Amalek, the villain who stalked the weakest of the ancient Israelites in the desert on their way to the Promised Land; the one that had been echoed by Amalek's ilk down through the generations; and the one that was now being shouted in mine—as my alarm bell. Those words would wake me up to the fact that I had spent much of my life on a holiday from history. And history, in a hail of bullets, had made its unequivocal return.

But this realization was to come. The morning of October 27, 2018, in a hotel room in Phoenix, I was pouring sweat and drinking lukewarm room-service coffee, replying to my editor at the *Times* to say yes, I would write a column immediately about what was going on.

This was before I learned that the name of the shooter was Robert Bowers, before I read what he had written on the social media website Gab: "There is no #MAGA as long as there is a kike infestation." It was before I knew he believed that the Jewish people were responsible for the sin of bringing Muslims to America: "Open you Eyes! It's the filthy EVIL jews Bringing the Filthy EVIL Muslims into the Country!!" Bowers hated the Hebrew Immigrant Aid Society, a Jewish organization founded in the late 1800s to resettle Jews fleeing pogroms in Russia and Eastern Europe. Today, it does the righteous work of rescuing Jews and non-Jews facing persecution all over the world. His final post before he entered the building was: "HIAS likes to bring invaders in that kill our people. I can't sit by and watch my people get slaughtered. Screw your optics, I'm going in." Tree of Life had been one of 270 synagogues around the country that had hosted National Refugee Shabbat the previous Saturday. That morning during services, American rabbis had spoken about the most fundamental and recurrent theme in the Bible: Do not oppress a stranger, because you were strangers in the land of Egypt.

This was before I stood in the sanctuary of the synagogue and watched an FBI agent named Nicholas Boshears break down in tears talking about what he'd witnessed in my community. Down the hall, his colleagues, in white coveralls, were cleaning and assessing what had become a crime scene: a chapel with hundreds of shell casings, dried rivers of blood, and tiny pieces of flesh.

It was before I sat with Rabbi Daniel Wasserman in his Squirrel Hill synagogue, Shaare Torah, his eyes wet and wide as he told me about what he'd seen. As a member of the community's *chevra kadisha*—literally, holy community—he was tasked with coordinating the cleanup of the bodies in accordance with Jewish law.

"I've seen bodies through *taharas*," he told me, referring to the ritual purification that takes place before a Jewish burial. "But unless someone is a medic in a battle zone or a soldier, I defy anyone to tell me they've seen that." It was, according to Robert Jones, the FBI special agent in charge of Pittsburgh, the "most horrific crime scene" he'd witnessed in twenty-two years.

Rabbi Wasserman had to shut off his brain so he could do his work. Even so, the images were burned there.

He told me he'd seen the dead body of a sweet, intellectually disabled man we both knew splayed at the entrance to the chapel. Cecil Rosenthal always came early to services with his brother, David, proud to serve as an usher and greet everyone who showed up with a prayer book and a wide smile. From the location of his corpse, it seemed that he had welcomed the killer, too.

Wasserman had seen Bernice and Sylvan Simon, who were married in that synagogue, dead in each other's arms. "He was protecting his wife," the rabbi said of the way their bodies were positioned. He shuddered as he told me about seeing a piece of a person's skull and recognizing immediately whose head it belonged to because he knew exactly how that man kept his hair.

This was before we knew all the names: the Rosenthals and the Simons and Joyce Fienberg and Richard Gottfried and Rose Mallinger and Jerry Rabinowitz and Daniel Stein and Melvin Wax and Irving Younger. It was before we buried them.

I filed the column that afternoon. Early the next morning, I gave the speech that had been my reason for coming to Phoenix. Someone sweet from the audience put a Pirates baseball cap on my head and I wore it as I walked through the airport.

Do you remember how things felt right after we watched the planes slam into the towers on September 11, 2001? I remember driving home from high school late that morning and noticing, as if in neon, the manicured lawns speeding by outside my window. I noticed that drivers stopped to let pedestrians cross and that the traffic lights worked and that the radio stations played. I remember realizing, maybe for the first time in my life, that none of it—not the paved roads or the running water or the loving parents who would come home from work to comfort me and my sisters—had to be that way. None of it was a guarantee.

That was how I felt walking through the Phoenix airport on October 28. I watched, baffled, as people told the cashier at Starbucks their coffee orders. I watched as one young woman asked another to borrow her cellphone charger. I watched as people lined up politely, according to their incomprehensibly assigned zone numbers, to board the plane, dragging their little wheeled suitcases behind them.

Everything was so miraculous. Everything was so fragile. The tears did not let up until I was thirty thousand feet above the country, heading back home to Pittsburgh.

. . .

I have always considered myself among the luckiest Jews in all of history.

This would be true simply if I had been born in America after the midcentury. These were the years of plenty for Jewish Americans. The hospitals and law firms Jews had built because they'd been shut out of the others were now the ones everyone was clamoring to join. The consummate outsiders had, in mere decades, become the insiders, capable of advocating not just for themselves but also for those still facing systemic discrimination—and all without having to give up smoked fish or Yom Kippur.

That I have lived in the United States at this time is a matter of incredible luck or blessing, depending on your belief in the otherworldly. But the reality I inherited was not a happy accident.

Most Americans my age do not know the name Charles Coughlin, but in the 1930s, thirty million Americans would tune in every week to listen to the priest who defended Kristallnacht and who said of the Jews: "We have lived to see the day that modern Shylocks have grown fat and wealthy, praised and deified, because they have perpetuated the ancient crime of usury under the modern racket of statesmanship." Coughlin was so influential that his town in Michigan had to build a new post office just to keep up with the nearly eighty thousand letters sent to him each week.

Henry Ford received a personal shout-out in *Mein Kampf* and was awarded, in 1938, the Grand Cross of the Supreme Order of the German Eagle, the highest honor the Nazis granted to any foreigner. Hitler, who owned a portrait of Ford, had been deeply inspired by the automaker's passionate Jew hatred, which was regularly articulated in Ford's newspaper, *The Dearborn Independent*.

In 1939, half a year before Hitler invaded Poland, more than twenty thousand people showed up at Madison Square Garden to rally for the Nazi cause with banners declaring, "Wake Up America. Smash Jewish Communism" and "Stop Jewish Domination of Christian Americans."

Anti-Semitism, in other words, wasn't just a German or European problem. The Jews of that continent were killed by the application of ideas—not just those in the minds of the masses shouting "Sieg Heil!" in Manhattan, but also the eugenics movement and Jim Crow—that were then also percolating in America.

A large measure of the American Jewish freedom I have enjoyed was a reaction to what happened in those bloodlands. The postwar, liberal America that rose as the Nazis fell became a fairer place to live for Jews because of the lessons that the world, and that America specifically, learned only after the murder of six million.

Of the Jews born into the two or three generations of the blessed, I had it even better than most. None of my grandparents had been in Europe during World War II. All had been born here. All met at the same public high school in Squirrel Hill, the neighborhood where my parents would later meet and, soon after, marry. Decades later, they still loved each other, despite (or maybe because of) the fact that they canceled out each other's votes. Every Friday night, our house became a salon over

Shabbat dinner as we debated politics and news and Judaism with ten guests or many more. They'd worked hard to make enough money to send me and my three sisters to Jewish day school and summer camp and programs in Israel.

And—crucially—I was born into an era in which all the doors that would have once kept me out of the rooms of the powerful had been pried open for me by tireless, angry, righteous feminists who insisted on women's fundamental equality. At least in theory, none of the barriers that had stood between my grandmother and her desires, or even between my mother and hers, were insurmountable for me.

I was raised in what can be accurately described as an urban shtetl. In Squirrel Hill, we looked out for one another. We knew we were far from the fanciest or the most sophisticated or really the most anything. But snobby was for other people. We were *haimish*—to use the Yiddish word for anything cozy, homey, and down-to-earth. It may as well be the Yiddish word for Pittsburgh.

I became a bat mitzvah at Tree of Life in March 1997—but the ceremony wasn't supposed to happen there. The previous October, a fire had blazed through my family's regular synagogue, Beth Shalom, less than a mile away. Jews and gentiles alike ran toward the fire. As Beth Shalom's executive director told a reporter at the time: "I didn't have to look. Everyone came to me." If that sounds like a Mister Rogers line, it may be because Squirrel Hill was literally his neighborhood.

• • •

A wise teacher once suggested to me that all of Jewish history—first set forth in the book of Exodus and then hammered home again after Hitler's genocide—teaches two lessons to the Jewish people. The first lesson is to survive. The second lesson is to never allow others to become slaves, because we know the bitterness of slavery, ancient and modern. It's a variation on the most famous phrase attributed to the first-century sage Rabbi Hillel: "If I am not for myself, who will be for me? But if I am only for myself, what am I? If not now, when?"

I never had to think about that first lesson; I was protected and privileged. Indeed, one of the gifts of the modern Jewish experience is that open-hearted Jewish values have almost entirely subsumed hard-headed ones because we have, by and large, been so welcomed here. Survival had no longer been our concern.

It's not that there weren't vestiges from an uglier, more violent past. There were jokes about picking up pennies and questions about horns. Then again, there were also snide comments from high school boys telling me to go back to the kitchen and make them a sandwich.

When I was in third or fourth grade, a Catholic school bus would swing by every morning while my sister and I were waiting at our bus stop. Some of the kids would pop their heads out of the windows and scream, "Kikes" and "Dirty Jews." My skin would burn up, and I would squeeze Casey's little hand tight. We had to ask our parents what "kike" meant; we'd never heard the slur. The screaming stopped the day my dad walked onto the bus and chewed out the kids. I don't remember being embarrassed when he did that.

Every branch of my family has the same portrait of my great-grandfather Chappy Goldstein. A poor immigrant, Chappy had been a professional flyweight boxer when he was a young man. In this official photo, a big Jewish star is emblazoned on his boxing shorts. I was proud to come from his stock, just as I was proud that my grandparents' store was threatened with a boycott because they supported the busing movement to integrate public schools in the 1970s. No great Torah scholars were in my lineage, as far as I knew. It was enough to have descended from tough Jews who did not back down from their principles.

From a very young age, I knew that we were the lucky ones and that things could be much worse. I knew that in part because we were a family of news junkies that talked about history. I also went to a school where we learned about people like Hannah Senesh (the Zionist Hungarian poet and paratrooper tortured and executed by the Nazis), and because every year on Yom HaShoah, survivors with numbers on their arms would come and tell us nightmares in broad daylight.

But I also knew things could be worse because I saw what was going on in other parts of the world. I saw the pictures of buses blown apart by suicide bombers in Jerusalem. I watched the YouTube video of Daniel Pearl when he said, "My father's Jewish, my mother's Jewish, I'm Jewish" before he was beheaded in Pakistan.

I was a student at Columbia University when I read about Ilan Halimi. At twenty-three, he was just a year older than me and lived in Paris, another of the most cosmopolitan cities in the world. He was healthy and good-looking and had Shabbat dinner every Friday night with his mother, Ruth, an immigrant from Morocco. On January 21, 2006, a group called the Gang of Barbarians—this is what they proudly called themselves—kidnapped Halimi because they assumed he had money. In fact, his divorced parents were of modest means and he had a job as a cellphone salesman. But the gang was sure he was rich because he was a Jew.

Over twenty-four days, they tortured this young man. They sent videos of the torture to his family. Halimi was found naked and handcuffed near the railroad tracks in Essonne, some fifteen miles south of Paris. He had been utterly mutilated: He had at least three stab wounds and the majority of his body had been burned with cigarettes and acid. He died in the ambulance on the way to the hospital.

Just as chilling as what the Gang of Barbarians did was the passionate refusal on the part of the French authorities to acknowledge the nature of the crime. "There isn't a single element allowing us to attach this murder to an anti-Semitic purpose or an anti-Semitic act," the investigative magistrate concluded in an official statement.

As the French writer Marc Weitzmann details powerfully in his new book *Hate*, the elements were, in fact, absolutely overwhelming. This was not a random kidnapping for ransom but a vicious hate crime carried out by a gang of more than twenty young people led by an unapologetic anti-Semite named Youssouf Fofana. But the cost of telling the truth was too high. It would mean admitting too much about the failure of France to protect its people; about its inability to assimilate Muslims; about the lawlessness of the suburbs; about the balkanization of French society; and, most of all, about the lethal power of anti-Jewish hate.

In the end, Ilan Halimi was murdered, and then he was sacrificed so as not to disturb France's illusions about itself.

. . .

Thirteen years later, those illusions have been shattered. This February, on the anniversary of Halimi's death, the tree in Paris planted in his memory was chopped down by anti-Semitic vandals. And the disease of the mind that drove Halimi's killers has spread and mutated across Europe.

The Jews of Paris have lived through the murders of Mireille Knoll, an eighty-five-year-old Holocaust survivor who was stabbed eleven times and then set on fire in her apartment, and, before her, of Sarah Halimi (no relation to Ilan), a sixty-five-year-old Jewish mother of three who was beaten to death and then thrown out her window. Toulouse, for French Jews, calls to mind the shooting at point-blank range of little children at the Ozar Hatorah school.

The Jews of Berlin know that you can be beaten for wearing a kippah or speaking Hebrew in public.

The Jews of Stockholm and Malmö know that when they enter a synagogue it might be firebombed.

The Jews of Brussels know that the Jewish Museum is not just a tourist site but a place where Jews were murdered.

The Jews of London know that Jeremy Corbyn, Labour's leader and the possible future prime minister of the United Kingdom, has described the genocidal terrorist groups Hamas and Hezbollah as his "friends."

The Jews of Warsaw just witnessed as the government of Poland—a place where there were once three million Jews and there are now fewer than ten thousand—passed a law making it illegal to say that the nation collaborated with the Nazis.

And this is to say nothing of the constant desecration of cemeteries; the demonization of Jews in the press and by politicians; the casual way that we are referred to as "apes and pigs" at anti-Israel rallies. On the streets of cities like London and Paris, Jews are cursed at, shoved, and spat upon. Some of them are my friends.

In 2019, with survivors of the Holocaust still walking the same streets where they were once rounded up, the reality is this: To be a public Jew—a religious Jew, a Zionist, or even a person with a Jewish last name or a Jewish-looking face—in several of the most refined European cities means, increasingly, to risk one's physical safety. It makes sense that so many Jews have chosen to live their lives partially in the closet. Some have removed physical signs: *mezuzot* from doorposts; *kippot* from heads; Magen Davids (Jewish stars) from necks. Others keep quiet about their views on any number of issues, but especially their feelings about Israel. A recent poll conducted by the European Union's Agency for Fundamental Rights found that 41 percent of Jews between the ages of sixteen and thiry-four have considered emigrating "because they did not feel safe living there as a Jewish person."

The Jews of Europe, as I noted in a November 2018 column in the *Times,* are trying to fight a kind of three-headed dragon. First, there is the physical fear of violent assault, often by young Islamist men, which leads many Jews to hide evidence of their religious identity. Second, there is moral fear of ideological vilification, mainly by the far left, which places sole blame for the continued conflict between Israel and the Palestinians on the Jewish state, and thus causes some Jews to downplay their sympathies for Israel or abandon it entirely. And third, there is profound political fear of resurgent fascism and populism, which can cause cognitive dissonance since at least some of Europe's neo-fascists and populists profess sympathy for Israel while expressing open hostility to Muslims.

The three threats often blend together, as they did recently in Paris when the public intellectual Alain

Finkielkraut was crossing the street and happened to walk by a group of Yellow Vest protestors who called him, variously, a "dirty Jew," a "Zionist shit," and a "fascist." They insisted: "Go home to Israel—to Tel Aviv!" Never mind that Finkielkraut is the son of Polish Holocaust survivors who were likely told the same thing.

I doubt that Finkielkraut's attackers knew much about the philosopher other than the fact of his Jewishness. I'm sure they didn't know that a few years ago, Finkielkraut was made a member of the Académie Française. Its forty members are referred to as the immortals—that is how important these people are to French culture—and Finkielkraut holds chair No. 21.

This attack on Finkielkraut puts me in mind of that chilling gaffe uttered in 1980 by Prime Minister Raymond Barre after a Jewish woman and three others were killed in a Paris synagogue bombing. "This despicable terrorist attack was aimed at Jews on their way to synagogue but hit innocent Frenchmen who were passing by," Barre said on live television. Here was the prime minister of France unwittingly telling his public that French Jews were somehow not entirely innocent, not entirely French, and thus were somehow a more appropriate target than the passersby. In aiming their bile at Alain Finkielkraut the Jew, as they will surely do again, the Yellow Vests inadvertently attacked a man who is the beating heart of French culture.

• • •

I had always thought it wasn't possible for this kind of cancer to metastasize in the United States, for three fundamental reasons.

One is the special nature of America. The United States, with its promise of free speech and religion, with its insistence that all people are created equal, with its tolerance for difference, with its emphasis on shared ideas rather than shared bloodline, has been, even with all of its ugly flaws, a New Jerusalem for the Jewish people.

This is a country whose first president, in 1790, wrote a letter to the Hebrew Congregation in Newport, Rhode Island, saying that the Jews of this country would "possess alike liberty of conscience and immunities of citizenship." He went on: "It is now no more that toleration is spoken of, as if it was by the indulgence of one class of people, that another enjoyed the exercise of their inherent natural rights." George Washington's radical proposition was that Jews would not be, as they always had been in history, second-class citizens in the new America. Rather, freedom would be as natural to the Jews as it was to any other citizen—at least as any other American then recognized as fully human. The Civil War, fought to make America's promise more real, was still seventy-one years away.

The reason Jews have thrived here as we have in no other diaspora in history is not coincidental. It is because of the nature of the country's founding vision. America's founders were in thrall to the "Old" Testament just as much as they were to the New. In that 1790 letter, as in so much of his writing, Washington quoted liberally from the Bible he knew so well. Here it was the prophet Micah, in a line that would later make its way into Lin-Manuel Miranda's score for *Hamilton:* "May the children of the stock of Abraham who dwell in this land continue to merit and enjoy the good will of the other inhabitants—while every one shall sit in safety under his own vine and fig tree and there shall be none to make him afraid."

The Puritans saw themselves as enacting a modern Exodus. They, too, were a small band of iconoclasts fleeing tyranny; they, too, had crossed a sea; they, too, were determined to worship their God freely in a promising land. So fully did they identify with the Israelites that Benjamin Franklin wanted the image on the country's great seal to be Moses parting the Red Sea. As Rabbi Meir Soloveichik pointed out in a brilliant 2018 lecture, America's founders, unlike Europe's, were "entranced with rather than envious of the miraculous story of the Jews and saw their own story not as replacing the biblical Israel but rather as reflecting it." It was Lincoln, as ever, who put it perfectly: Americans, he said, were the "almost chosen people."

All this is why, as the German writer Josef Joffe has noted, "America is dotted with biblical place names like Jerusalem, Shiloh, Zion, Canaan, and Goshen." And yet "there is no Shiloh anywhere in Europe."

The second reason I believed that it would be impossible for anti-Semitism to flourish in this country and in

ady of anti-Semitism. My primary goal here is to wake us up, to help us recover what Fest's father rightly feared his friends had forgotten. If the bloody years that followed his warning offered incontrovertible proof of anything, it's that what starts with the Jews never ends with them.

I do not think the best use of any minority's time and attention is to focus on its haters. But I think it is essential to understand and analyze this disease of the mind, in its various permutations, because to understand anti-Semitism is to inoculate oneself against an ideology that cannot withstand critical thinking. Understanding it is also the beginning of fighting it. And we need to fight it.

It is important, here at the outset, to grasp the stakes of this struggle. The object of our protection is not just the Jewish people. It is the health and future of a country that promised to be a New Jerusalem for all who sought it out.

I know that much of what I write here will not win me fans, not least among those quietists in my own community who think the solution to our present problems is to work behind the scenes, to join boards, to create ever more dialogue groups to process and workshop and circle back and build consensus and move the needle over long years and decades. If they are lucky. Nor will it win me praise from those fearful of being pilloried for having the wrong views by those they imagine are more enlightened.

So be it.

This book is for anyone, Jew or gentile, who is concerned not with what is fashionable but with what is true.

This book is for anyone, Jew or gentile, who loves freedom and seeks to protect it. It is for anyone, Jew or gentile, who cannot look away from what is brewing in this country and in the world and wants to do something to stop it.

That a Jew would see a storm threatening and write to warn of its gathering is not new. But it is an old tradition that I did not think would need to be taken up in this new century.

Yet here I am—a Jew, an American, a Zionist, a proud daughter of Pittsburgh—raising the old-new cry with all my might and hoping that you will hear in its call something that will give you no other choice but to take up this fight.

CHAPTER 2

A BRIEF HISTORY

Any serious fight must begin by sizing up one's opponent. What are her strengths? Her vulnerabilities? Her style of combat? Who has managed to beat her and who has succumbed?

Anti-Semitism is fueled by the malicious but often feeds on the ignorance of the well-intentioned. Battling it means being able to accurately recognize and describe it.

The first problem in understanding anti-Semitism is that this particular enemy is not a person or even a set of people. It is not even a solid idea or a singular theory. It is a shape-shifting worldview that slithers away just as you think you have it pinned down and, in so doing, stays several steps ahead of anyone trying to clobber it.

The second problem is that it is unclear what this protean worldview actually opposes. Sometimes it seems bent on eliminating a religion. At other times, it seeks to erase a culture or destroy a particular group of people or eradicate a state. This leads to further complication: What exactly is the anti-Semite attacking? Put another way: What exactly is Judaism?

Most Americans, including many American Jews, understand Judaism as a religion or as an ethnicity because these are the modern categories by which we understand much of the world. Christianity is a faith. Latino is an ethnicity. And so forth. But Judaism (and the force that opposes it, which today we call anti-Semitism) greatly predates and thus does not fit any of these far more recently constructed categories, despite how aggressively some try to shoehorn it into them.

Judaism is not merely a religion, and it is not merely an ethnicity. Judaism is a people. More specifically, it is a people with a language, a culture, a literature, and a particular set of ideas, beliefs, texts, and legal practices. One word for that is a civilization. Another is a tribe. Yet try identifying yourself as a member of a tribe these days and, quite understandably, you'll get a furrowed brow in reply.

To a great extent, this gross misunderstanding about Judaism can be seen as a result of the happy fact that the Jews have been so widely accepted in the United States. Many American Jews themselves lack any real historical understanding of where they come from. They'll check a box saying that Judaism is a religion. They might describe themselves as a people with a particular passion for Jerry Seinfeld and hummus. That's true as far as it goes. But it doesn't go very far.

In normal times, this misunderstanding about the definition of Judaism and the Jewish people is not high-stakes. It's okay that it remains obscure because it has little bearing on anyone's day-to-day life. In times of rising anti-Semitism, however, it begins to matter a great deal. Because you cannot defend yourself against something if you have only a vague understanding of who you are and what you're fighting for.

Consider the common misunderstanding these days that anti-Semitism is a form of racism. One reason that anti-Semitism is understood as racism against Jews is because racism is at the center of America's conversation with itself. The greatest shame and injustice in American history was slavery; the greatest righting of a wrong was its abolition; and among our greatest contemporary struggles is persistent racial inequality.

What's more, Jews have always bent toward and adopted the cultural mores of the societies of which they are a part. We have been willing, wittingly or unwittingly, to inscribe our own history and our own identity in a somewhat distorted form as a way of being understandable to our neighbors. Thus in some contexts, we have allowed ourselves to be understood as a religion. Here, often, we have allowed ourselves to be understood as an ethnicity.

The trouble is that if anti-Semitism is a form of racism

against a minority group and if Jews in the United States are largely thought of as white, then the contemporary question about American Jews is: Where do they rank in the hierarchy of racial oppression?

The answer—perfectly logically—is way toward the bottom. This is true historically: Were there laws in Maryland saying that Jews couldn't hold public office? Yes. Was that the same as human beings in the Old Line State being bought and sold as property? Absolutely not. And it is true in the present day: Are Jews barred from some country clubs? Yes. But are Jews singled out and discriminated against, not least by law enforcement, because of an immutable physical characteristic? Most definitely not. If anti-Semitism is simply a subcategory of racism, then, by American standards, it is, rightly, far less acute than racism against black people. And, therefore, it is a less urgent priority.

Calling anti-Semitism a form of racism is problematic in other ways, not least of which is that it whitewashes the Jewish people. It ignores the fact that more than half of Israel's Jews, the biggest Jewish community in the world, are Mizrahi (of North African and Middle Eastern descent). And it overlooks the reality that 12 to 15 percent of American Jews are people of color, according to the Jews of Color Field Building Initiative.

There is such a thing as anti-Jewish prejudice, of course. And this prejudice presents itself much like racial prejudice. This is the prejudice that kept our grandparents out of the Ivy League; that moved them to change their last names; and so on. While anti-Jewish prejudice is offensive and inconvenient and painful in the lives of individual Jews, it makes little significant difference in the survival of Judaism and the Jewish people. Anti-Semitism, which has as its ultimate goal the elimination of Judaism and the Jewish people, does.

Here's one way to think about it: Anti-Jewish prejudice might mean that a gentile prefers that his daughter doesn't marry a Jew. But it does not mean that he believes that the Jews are a nefarious force that secretly exerts control over our government. That's anti-Semitism. Anti-Jewish prejudice might lead a non-Jewish couple to hope that Jews don't move in next door. But it does not mean they believe that Jewish bankers manipulate the global economy. That's anti-Semitism. And, these days, a quite common expression of it.

If anti-Semitism is not merely a kind of prejudice, though it can have similar effects, *what is it?*

Jean-Paul Sartre, in his famous essay "Anti-Semite and Jew," insists that anti-Semitism does not operate by the normal rules of logic, but "derives from the logic of passion." Peter Hayes, a historian of the Holocaust, has smartly explained it as "a kind of superstition," as baseless but as enduring as knocking on wood. I think of it as an ever-morphing conspiracy theory in which Jews play the starring role in spreading evil in the world.

While racists or homophobes or misogynists see themselves as punching down, anti-Semites often perceive themselves as punching up. In the eyes of the racist, the person of color is inferior. In the eyes of the misogynist, the woman is something less than human. In the eyes of the anti-Semite, the Jew is . . . everything. He is whatever the anti-Semite needs him to be.

Anti-Semitism successfully turns Jews into the symbol of whatever a given civilization defines as its most sinister and threatening qualities. When you look through this dark lens, you can understand how, under communism, the Jews were the capitalists. How under Nazism, the Jews were the race contaminators. And today, when the greatest sins are racism and colonialism, Israel, the Jew among the nations, is being demonized as the last bastion of white, racist colonialism—a unique source of evil not just in the region but in the world. Whatever role "the Jews" are needed for, well, that is the part they are forced to play.

The logic of anti-Semitism is very different from the logic of xenophobia or racism. It is not just a form of hatred, one that happens to be directed against Jews rather than against lesbians or Koreans or left-handed people. It is a grand unified theory of everything. As the father of modern French anti-Semitism, Edouard Drumont, put it in his 1886 book *La France juive,* three years before he founded his country's Anti-Semitic League: "All comes from the Jew; all returns to the Jew."

Racists don't believe that people with more melanin are secretly controlling the planet; they believe they are subhuman. Both sets of beliefs are hideous and paranoid. Only one is a global conspiracy theory.

Perhaps the British historian Paul Johnson captures it most accurately when he calls anti-Semitism an intellectual disease. It is a deeply rooted and highly infectious thought virus carried in the DNA of Western culture. This may sound terrifying and deterministic. But extend the metaphor and it becomes a bit less so. Healthy people carry many, many viruses all the time. If you are healthy, you harbor these viruses inside yourself without any symptoms. It is only when you are under severe stress that your immune system falters and you start to get sick. And then the virus, which had been dormant, begins to reveal itself.

Likewise in our culture. When our society's immune system is healthy and functioning normally, the virus of anti-Semitism is kept in check. But when our social immune system is weakened—as it is right now, and dramatically so—the virus will out, as it has so many times before in some of the most seemingly civilized cultures on the planet.

．　．　．

The anti-Semitic disease we encounter today in the United States and in the West more generally is the result of thousands of years of mutations.

Others far wiser and more knowledgeable than I have written books about each iteration of the anti-Semitic disease. (Bernard Lewis's *Semites and Anti-Semites* is particularly indispensable.) My focus here is on its present manifestations. To the Hasidic Jew getting beaten by young men in Crown Heights, or the Jewish college student served an eviction notice in her dorm by anti-Zionist activists, or the rabbi now missing a finger because it was shot off by a teenage neo-Nazi, the particular strain of this disease motivating their tormentors doesn't much matter. Regardless of what was in the heart or mind of the anti-Semite, the Jew still has a bloody nose.

I think here of the Dahan family, who in 2014 moved from Sderot, Israel, to Mira Mesa, California, to escape the constant Hamas rockets launched from the nearby Gaza Strip. During the Dahans' first Passover in America, swastikas were painted on their garage. For a time, the family of five all slept in a single locked room with knives and baseball bats. Then, in April 2019, eight-year-old Noya Dahan went to the Chabad of Poway on the last day of Passover and left with shrapnel in her leg and her cheek. Her uncle, visiting from Israel, was shot in the leg. "We came from fire to fire," Israel Dahan, Noya's father, said of their situation. In one instance, the terrorist was a white supremacist. In another, the terrorists were Islamists. Both wanted to do the same thing to the Dahan family.

Or I think of the Reijnen family. The Reijnens left Rotterdam, where anti-Semitism had become a regular feature of life, and moved to Israel because, they believe, "life is better in Israel for our children. We are Jewish and we want to live in a Jewish community." The family now lives at Kibbutz Nahal Oz, half a mile from Gaza. This

May, they were officially initiated into the neighborhood when their home was hit by a rocket launched from the Strip. In the end, anti-Semitism, no matter its source, has the same fate in mind for Jews.

Yet to wake ourselves up to the violence experienced by families like these, we need to look briefly at what we have inherited in our cultural DNA.

. . .

The roots of anti-Semitism are ancient and located in the same place where the Israelites were enslaved: Egypt. Scholars place much of the blame on a pagan—an Egyptian priest by the name of Manetho. His original anti-Semitic conspiracy theory, devised in about 300 B.C.E., was a response to the Jewish story of the Exodus at a time when Alexandria's Jewish community was the largest in the world. Manetho's story was quite different from the biblical narrative, in which God liberated the Israelites, bringing them out of Egyptian slavery to freedom. The priest insisted that the Jews of Egypt were actually lepers who had taken control of Egypt and unleashed a reign of terror on its people. Egypt was saved only thanks to an exiled Egyptian king who killed the diseased Jews and banished the remaining ones from his land.

According to Professor Moshe Sharon of Hebrew University, "Manetho's story was designed to negate everything positive about the Jews." In the Bible, the Jews are a people with distinct ethics and beliefs. Here they are lepers. In the Bible, an all-powerful God capable of parting a sea frees the slaves because he has chosen them. In Manetho's revisionist story, they are summarily expelled by a king.

It wasn't just the radical story of the Exodus that bothered these early Egyptians. In his brilliant book *Anti-Judaism,* the University of Chicago professor David Nirenberg writes about a decree issued by King Darius II more than one hundred years before Manetho. In the decree, the king ordered the Egyptians of Elephantine to stay away from the Jews during Passover, the annual festival celebrating the Israelites' liberation. Why? Many scholars think that the Egyptian priests were offended by the ritual Jewish Passover offering of the lamb. It's an explanation that makes good sense, given that the Egyptians worshipped a ram-god.

But Nirenberg offers an answer that I think is more convincing, even if it suggests a deeper civilizational clash. "The Egyptians were offended not only by the sacrifice but also by the very nature of the Passover festival as a reenactment of the Exodus from Egypt," he writes. "What was for the Jews a commemoration of liberation and of the victory of monotheism over idolatry, was for the Egyptians an offensive celebration of the destruction of Egypt and the defeat of its gods."

The sacrifice, in other words, wasn't the primary problem. The problem was that the radical story of the Exodus undermined the entire ideological structure of Egyptian culture. The Jewish story exposed Egypt's idols and gods as powerless. The Jewish story exposed slavery as evil and insisted on human freedom. Hundreds of years before Jesus was born, the Jews were conscripted in a war of religious and cultural ideas.

Early Christianity shifted the battlefield. If in Egypt the Jews rejected paganism, now the Jews were the people who not only rejected their own Messiah but who conspired with the Roman Empire to have him killed. Indeed, the story outlined in the Gospels is the template for a conspiracy theory of the Jews as nefarious manipulators that continues to be expressed today: the ability of a tiny minority to use its wiles and its proximity to power to con others into accomplishing its evil ends.

After all, in the New Testament it is a small group of seemingly powerless Jews who cajole Rome, then the greatest power in the world, to do their bidding and kill Christ. Pontius Pilate, the Roman governor, speaks to the Jews about Jesus in the book of John: "Take him yourselves and judge him according to your own law." But the Jews punt the decision back to Pilate: "We are not permitted to put anyone to death." And so Pilate does the deed on their behalf.

In the book of Matthew, the implications of this manipulation are spelled out: "His blood is on us and our children," the Jews say—a line that has been so historically destructive that even the unrepentant anti-Semite Mel Gibson did not translate it in the English subtitles of his film *The Passion of the Christ*, though it is spoken in Aramaic. (Not for nothing: The Pittsburgh killer cited

John 8:44 on Gab, writing "Jews are the children of satan.")

The rationale for demonizing the Jews must have seemed logical to the early evangelists, just as later it was logical for Islam to change the direction Muslims face when they pray after the Jewish tribes of Medina rejected the Prophet Mohammed. Both the evangelists and the Muslims were trying to separate themselves from Judaism while building on its foundations. To create a new phenomenon and to distinguish it from an older tradition, they had to draw bright lines. The mere fact that the Jews continued to exist in the world as Jews was an affront to the most foundational Christian idea, which is that the Messiah had indeed come.

My intent here is not to blame thousands of years of Christian doctrine—not at all—or to suggest that because Western civilization grew out of these roots, it is somehow fundamentally doomed. It is simply to point out the historical and intellectual depth of the anti-Jewish conspiracy. If the Christian Bible is the most important book in Western civilization and Jesus is that civilization's most important figure, the Jews' rejection of him and his message means that anti-Semitism is baked into the very foundations of the world we inhabit.

The old anti-Semitic line, which has since been reclaimed by some Jews as a dark joke, goes like this: If everyone hates the Jews, maybe they're doing something wrong. For the anti-Semite, the "maybe" there is superfluous—obviously they are. But the anti-Semite's answer also, inadvertently, contains some truth. The Jews *are* doing something. Not something wrong, of course, but something different. The iconoclastic ideas that drove Egyptians to create a revisionist history remain iconoclastic thousands of years later. The bad-good news is that the radical nature of the Jewish story still has the power to drive people crazy.

. . .

Jews had no political power in the many centuries that followed the death of Jesus and the destruction of the Second Temple in Jerusalem by the Romans in 70 C.E. They could not own land; they were barred from most professions; they could not hold public office or marry outside the tribe. And yet, over and over again, they stood accused of new variations of working with the Romans to kill Christ—of pulling the levers of power and sowing terror in the societies in which they were actually second-class citizens.

I could use up a thousand pages detailing each of these conspiracies and the bloodshed that followed. Consider just one example: In the 1300s, the real culprits of the bubonic plague, which swept through Europe and killed tens of millions of people, were rats that had come to the continent via ship from Crimea. But Jews were blamed for spreading the disease by poisoning drinking wells. Some historians say that Jews were, in fact, succumbing to the plague at a rate lower than their neighbors. Likely this was because their religious rituals—washing hands before eating bread; bathing before Shabbat—were also hygienic and made them less susceptible to the disease.

No one thought to mimic the practices of the Jews. Instead, there were massacres in more than sixty Jewish communities throughout Europe. On January 9, 1349, nearly the entire Jewish community of Basel, Switzerland, was forced into a big wooden house on an island in the Rhine River. It had been constructed specifically for the occasion. There, in that wooden house, six hundred souls were burned alive. The few Jews who were spared were children who'd been forcibly converted.

By the fifteenth century, Jewishness, according to our enemies, was becoming something that could not be wiped away even by conversion. Religious anti-Semitism was morphing. Now it was a matter of blood more than belief. During the Spanish Inquisition, converted Jews were not even called Christians; they were referred to as Conversos, since they could never be considered fully Christian. Something about them could never be entirely assimilated. Race was a notion centuries from being conceptualized, but the seeds of the racial anti-Semitism that the Nazis later perfected were planted in this fateful period.

Dip into the major events of any of the centuries that followed—or look into most of the boldface names—and you will find traces of this rapidly evolving disease.

In high school I learned that Martin Luther was the genius behind the Protestant Reformation, the man who stood up to the all-powerful Catholic Church. But I did not learn that when the Jews refused to adopt his Christianity, he turned viciously against them. In a 1543 pamphlet, *The Jews and Their Lies,* he calls the Jews "venomous, bitter, vindictive, tricky serpents, assassins, and children of the devil" and offers some policy recommendations for dealing with such scum. "Set fire to their synagogues or schools" to "honor" God so that "God might see that we are Christians." Their homes should be "razed and destroyed" and "all their prayer books and Talmudic writings, in which such idolatry, lies, cursing, and blasphemy are taught, be taken from them."

The Enlightenment may have unseated God and the power of the church, but it was not always the Age of Reason. In the eighteenth and nineteenth centuries, the religious hatred against the Jews morphed again. Now it was possible to be an anti-Semite without any religious justification at all. This was the advent of social, political, and nationalistic anti-Semitism.

In 1771, less than twenty years before George Washington wrote to the Jews of Rhode Island with biblical assurances, and before the hyperrational fanaticism of the French Revolution devoured his own country in blood, Voltaire, who would come to define the Enlightenment, wrote this of the Jewish people: "They are, all of them, born with raging fanaticism in their hearts, just as the Bretons and the Germans are born with blond hair. I would not be in the least bit surprised if these people would not some day become deadly to the human race."

In 1789, the same year that the United States Constitution went into effect, the revolutionary Clermont-Tonnerre, speaking in a debate about the status of Jews in the new French nation, laid the foundations for the idea that our religious faith could be separated from our sense of peoplehood: "We must refuse everything to the Jews as a nation and accord everything to the Jews as individuals. . . . It is repugnant to have in the state an association of non-citizens, and a nation within the nation."

In 1843, less than a hundred years before the attempt to rid the world of capitalism unleashed a mass murder so enormous that its victims are still being counted, Marx wrote in "On the Jewish Question": "In the final analysis, the *emancipation of the Jews* is the emancipation of mankind from *Judaism*."

By the time the Nazis and the Communists came around, anti-Semitism did not require any religion at all. These secular anti-Semitic movements murdered more Jews than any religious anti-Semites ever had.

Even the term "anti-Semitism" speaks to the ever-evolving nature of the anti-Jewish conspiracy. Wilhelm Marr, a German activist and journalist, popularized the term in his 1879 pamphlet "The Victory of Judaism over Germandom." The word that had previously been used to describe anti-Jewish sentiment was *Judenhass*, or "Jew hatred." As Deborah Lipstadt writes in her book

Antisemitism Here and Now, the word was not sufficient because even Jews who converted could not convert out of their essential nature, their essential otherness. Marr's new coinage, *Antisemitismus,* or "Antisemitism," she notes, "had a racial and 'scientific' connotation rather than a religious one."

Lipstadt renders the word without the hyphen—"antisemitism"—as a way to signify that there is no way to be anti-Semitic as one is anti-vaccine or anti-abortion, because Semitism itself is a construct, a fake category, originally used to describe a group of languages that originated in the Near East.

David Nirenberg has suggested that "anti-Semitism" is far too narrow a term because it speaks only to bigotry against Jewish people, not bigotry against Jewish ideas. It fails to explain why, even in cultures where there were few or no Jews at all, they were still hated so intensely. Because this phenomenon is not primarily about Jewish individuals but about the very idea of Judaism, of Jewishness, and of Jewish peoplehood, he argues that the term "anti-Judaism" is a far better way of describing what he sees as essential scaffolding for Western civilization. "Anti-Judaism should not be understood as some archaic or irrational closet in the vast edifices of Western thought. It was rather one of the basic tools with which that edifice was constructed," he writes.

Nirenberg is entirely right about the expansive and ideological nature of the problem. But I continue to call this conspiracy theory "anti-Semitism" because I want to be well and widely understood. When I use it, however, I'm not referring merely to prejudice against Jewish individuals. I mean it to describe a culturally inherited disease that cannot be remedied with one round of antibiotics.

With this in mind, it's not surprising that in 1894, when a French army captain by the name of Alfred Dreyfus was falsely accused of passing military secrets to Germany, "Death to the Jews" was chanted in the streets. Nor should it come as a shock that in 1903, when the czarist secret police published the fake minutes of a meeting of Jewish power brokers, *The Protocols of the Elders of Zion*, masses of people believed it was true. Or that now, decades after it has been revealed as a Russian forgery, the screed remains a bestseller in countries like Egypt.

If you look back to the 1970s, when the Soviet Union sponsored a United Nations resolution declaring that Zionism was racism—put forth because its client countries had failed to destroy the State of Israel—you can now see that for what it was: anti-Semitism morphing once again, drawing on its ancient roots while hijacking modern language of good and evil.

When right-wing populists in Europe and here at home accuse the Jews of betraying the dominant Christian culture by supporting immigrants and other minorities, you will hear the chants of those Nazi supporters who gathered in Madison Square Garden in February 1939 from beyond the grave. And when leftists slip effortlessly from criticizing the settlement enterprise to suggesting that the Jewish state is a racist one that should not exist, you will know they are unknowingly parroting a piece of Soviet propaganda.

. . .

If anti-Semitism is a conspiracy theory without grounding in reality, is there any way to predict when it will rear its head? The rule of thumb is that anti-Semitism rises at times of great insecurity and upheaval. When there is unrest or inexplicable change, the Jew is often blamed. It's not a coincidence, to choose the most obvious example, that Germany in the 1920s and 1930s was experiencing a severe economic depression.

The problem with this kind of logic is that it can risk excusing anti-Semitism. It may well be that the leader of the Cossack rebellion in Ukraine in the mid-1600s, Bohdan Khmelnytsky, was genuinely frustrated by oppressive Polish rule and wanted a state for his own people. But that does not explain the hideous bloodletting now known by his name in which, by most estimates, some one hundred thousand Jews were slaughtered. These were massacres in which, according to a contemporary account by Rabbi Nathan Hannover, the wombs of pregnant women were sliced open, the babies ripped out and replaced with live cats. Then the women's hands were cut off so that they could not remove the cats inside their bodies.

There are often proximate materialist "reasons" for

anti-Semitism. But to suggest that a society reaches for it in particular moments says nothing about actual Jews and Judaism and everything about the health of that society. Today, alas, the culture we live in is increasingly grasping for it.

On the far right, Jews are condemned as internationalists, disparaged for being insufficiently white and for refusing to renounce universalist values. This anti-Semitism is an anti-globalism that regurgitates many of the oldest anti-Semitic tropes even as it pretends to be fervently pro-Israel. The second kind comes from the far left, which denies Jewish peoplehood and our right to self-determination by treating Israel as a uniquely diabolical state. Anti-Zionist anti-Semitism cloaks itself in the language of progressive values—standing up for the downtrodden, protecting the underdog—even as anti-Zionists make common cause with some of the most regressive ideologies and regimes on earth. Both types position the Jews as a people apart, a people arrayed against the interests of "the people."

In the *Jewish Review of Books,* the writer Dara Horn points out that the two threats we face today are, in fact, very ancient ones that go back to two important Jewish holidays: Purim and Hanukkah. All anti-Semitism, she argues, can be divided into Purim anti-Semitism and Hanukkah anti-Semitism.

"In the Purim version, exemplified by the Persian genocidal decrees in the biblical book of Esther, as well as by more recent ideologies like Nazism and today's many versions of radical Islam, the regime's goal is unambiguous: Kill all the Jews," Horn writes. "In the Hanukkah version, as in the 2nd-century B.C.E. Hellenized Seleucid regime that criminalized all expressions of Judaism, the goal is still to eliminate Jewish civilization."

That's the rub with Hanukkah anti-Semitism. It asks the Jews to take part in their own destruction. That's why "the Hanukkah version of anti-Semitism—whose appearances range from the Spanish Inquisition to the Soviet regime—often employs Jews as its agents," Horn writes. "These 'converted' Jews openly renounce whatever aspects of their Jewish identity are unacceptable to the relevant regime, proudly declare their loyalty to the ideology of the day, and loudly urge other Jews to follow them. These people are used as cover to demonstrate the good intentions of the regime—which of course isn't anti-Semitic, but merely requires that its Jews publicly flush thousands of years of Jewish civilization down the toilet in exchange for the prize of not being treated like dirt or murdered. For a few years. Maybe."

Today, Purim anti-Semitism, as always, is clear and easy to spot. It is the Pittsburgh killer. It is Iran. It is Hamas officials like Fathi Hamad, who called on the Palestinian diaspora to murder Jews this summer: "All of you seven million Palestinians abroad, enough of the warming up. You have Jews everywhere and we must attack every Jew on the globe by way of slaughter and killing, if God permits." Hanukkah anti-Semitism, which asks the Jews to commit cultural genocide, to abandon their traditions and to worship false idols to survive, is more insidious. You see manifestations of this tragic strain in what has become of the British Labour Party and in the activist and academic left in the United States. In the chapters that follow, I will examine each of these iterations of this ancient malady, as well as the anti-Semitism of radical Islam, which combines toxic elements of both.

Remember: It is easy to think of the Jews as the sole victims of anti-Semitic hate. But another, far bigger victim is often overlooked: the culture that facilitates anti-Semitism. To tolerate anti-Semitism is to tolerate lies. A culture in which anti-Semitism thrives is a culture in which truths have been replaced with lies.

Think back to Ilan Halimi. The French police and French politicians and the French press had to lie about every aspect of what his murder was and what it meant in order to maintain the fictions they were telling themselves about French society.

Indeed, if you examine societies that have embraced anti-Semitism, you will see that they have gone mad because they have substituted a conspiracy theory for reality. We, too, have started to descend into madness.

CHAPTER 3

THE RIGHT

Growing up, I listened carefully when my grandfather talked about America. He always insisted that this country was his promised land. A poor Jewish kid raised by a single mother, he went on to achieve what we used to unironically call the American dream.

My grandpa Jack's view was not unique: Generations of Eastern European immigrants called this place the *goldene medinah*, literally the "golden land." Even as we have adapted, over the past decades, to armed guards at our Jewish Community Centers and metal detectors at our synagogues, I don't think we ever fully believed that these measures were anything but a precaution. Jews in other countries had real reason to fear killing sprees that targeted Jewish schools and places of worship. We were different.

Then came Pittsburgh. The message I heard from community leaders and rabbis in my hometown and across the country was that the slaughter should not change our assessment of this country. It was a one-off. America was still what we thought it was.

That was what they insisted. Until April 27.

For the second time in American history, Jews were shot dead as they prayed in synagogue, this time in Poway, California, on the last day of Passover, the Jewish festival of freedom.

Again, a weapon of war, purchased legally, was used to hunt people down in a house of worship. Again, ordinary people showed extraordinary courage. Again, the press swarmed the town. Again, a shattered community buried its dead. Again, there were candlelight vigils and Twitter hashtags and GoFundMe drives. Again, there were emails and op-eds expressing shock and outrage and heartbreak. Again, we promised: Never again.

Never again until Monday rolled around, when the news broke that the FBI had arrested Mark Steven Domingo, a twenty-six-year-old army veteran who had converted to Islam and said he was inspired by ISIS. According to the federal affidavit, Domingo considered planning several attacks, "including targeting Jews, churches, and police officers." He had purchased especially long nails to ensure maximum internal organ damage when his bombs exploded.

This particular April felt like the cruelest month: Three black churches were burned in Louisiana, the alleged work of a white arsonist. A man named Isaiah Peoples, an African American army veteran, now faces eight counts of attempted murder for plowing his car into a group of people because they were Muslim. Four members of a Sikh family were shot dead in their Ohio home in a possible hate crime. On top of these horrors is the "random" gun violence, the bullets aimed at any living human, without discrimination. The eight people shot in Baltimore on a Sunday afternoon. The two dead and four injured college students at the University of North Carolina at Charlotte. It is hard to recount all the disgusting details.

Contrary to my grandfather's insistence, and the soothing assurances of community leaders, it was clear after the Poway attack that Jews—never mind everyone else living in a divided nation awash in weapons owned by people who could radicalize themselves in front of computer screens—had reason to be afraid in America.

What if the Shining City on a Hill had morphed into a country riven by hate, where mass public killings with automatic weapons had become a sick, competitive spectacle, to be replayed on cable news shows and the fever swamps of virtual message boards? And what if the history of the Jews in America wasn't a straight line, moving ever more gloriously toward greater heights of comfort and achievement and understanding, but a pendulum, which had swung one way and was now swinging back, into the darkness of the Old World that my grandparents' generation was sure they'd left behind?

. . .

John Earnest, the man arrested for pulling the trigger of an AR-15 and killing Lori Gilbert-Kaye in her San Diego–area synagogue, is not special in his hatred. Earnest, who has pled not guilty, shares a worldview with Pittsburgh killer Robert Bowers and Brenton Tarrant, the Australian who murdered fifty-one Muslims as they prayed in their New Zealand mosques on March 15, 2019. All are captive minds that worship the false god of whiteness.

These sick murderers—and their legions of anonymous fanboys lurking on message boards like 8chan and 4chan—are fueled by a belief in white supremacy. Even more to the point, they are gripped by a fear of "whiteness" being muddied and diluted and eventually washed away by waves of non-white, non-Christian Americans and immigrants—a takeover engineered, of course, by devious Jews, who manipulate governments through their control of banks, Hollywood, the media, and even borders themselves.

To spend too much time parsing the barely coherent online ranting of these killers, punctuated by in-jokes designed to prank the police and the media in search of an "explanation" for their actions, is to fall into the trap they have set. Their ironic quips and their memes don't actually matter. What matters is that these people want to kill those who threaten their vision of "white America." Especially Jews.

I have zero desire to live in their world. But the truth was that even before the Pittsburgh slaughter, I already did. After all, before Earnest and Bowers, there was Timothy McVeigh, who blew up the Alfred P. Murrah Federal Building in Oklahoma City, killing 168 people and wounding over 680 more. Before McVeigh there was a Christian identitarian group called The Order, which went on a rampage of robberies, bombings, and assassinations throughout the West in the 1980s. In 1959, George Lincoln Rockwell founded the American Nazi Party, which was itself a vestige of other American pro-Nazi organizations like the Silver Shirts and the German American Bund. In the 1920s, hooded Ku Klux Klan mobs lynched and murdered black Americans with the seeming approval of local and state governments. (The group had more than two million members at the time.)

If the neo-Nazis and the Christian identitarians—those, like Earnest, who combine classical medieval anti-Semitism with American white supremacy—are the especially violent ones, they are also part of the penumbra of bigots and loners, haters and losers, online mischief makers and real-world brawlers, who are collectively known as the alt-right. They are the people who gathered in a park in Charlottesville in August 2017 for the Unite the Right protest and fought running battles with the police as they chanted their white supremacist bile.

For all of the media attention these people have received, they remain the most socially marginalized anti-Semites in America, many banned from Twitter and Facebook, others living in their parents' homes, such as the organizer of the Charlottesville protest, Jason Kessler. But America has never had any shortage of these anti-Semites, some of them quite powerful and prominent people who viewed my grandfather's dream with loathing, and saw Jews not as Americans but as a threat to what America ought to be.

Early in the twentieth century, Leo Frank, a Jewish factory manager in Atlanta, was convicted of the murder of a thirteen-year-old worker named Mary Phagan in a series of trials that more closely resembled medieval blood libels than modern legal proceedings. Frank was sentenced to death. But after the governor of Georgia commuted Frank's sentence to life in prison, a gang of around twenty-five men calling themselves the Knights of Mary Phagan took Frank from prison. On the morning of August 17, 1915, they lynched him. More than half of the three thousand Jews then living in Georgia left the state.

Henry Ford, who along with Thomas Edison was the great hero of machine age America, was also a virulent anti-Semite who paid for hundreds of thousands of copies of *The Protocols of the Elders of Zion* to be printed and distributed across the country, including in schools. Ford's newspaper, *The Dearborn Independent,* was a primary source of anti-Semitic conspiracy theories that blamed Jews for, among other things, engineering World War I for profit. The Jews were the enemy of world peace, Ford and his propagandists instructed.

In the 1930s, self-styled "Silver Shirts" and other followers of Adolf Hitler paraded down the streets of American cities and towns with swastika armbands and held mass rallies in places like Madison Square Garden, while Father Coughlin railed against the Jews' conspiracy to communize America through their control of Franklin Roosevelt and to plunge the world into another war. In 1938, weeks before Kristallnacht, the celebrated American aviator Charles Lindbergh was presented with a Nazi medal by Hermann Göring in Berlin. Three years later, the staunch isolationist gave a speech before eight thousand in Des Moines called "Who Are the War Agitators?" in which he declared, "The three most important groups who have been pressing this country toward war are the British, the Jewish, and the Roosevelt administration."

In the 1950s, the KKK bombed and shot up Jewish synagogues in the South, in a wave of anti-Semitic violence that blamed Jews for their support of the civil rights movement. In October 1958, fifty sticks of dynamite exploded in Atlanta's oldest Reform synagogue, which was helmed by a rabbi who was an outspoken opponent of segregation. All five of the suspects were members of anti-Semitic groups like the National States' Rights Party and the Knights of the White Camelia. In September 1967, Congregation Beth Israel in Jackson, Mississippi, was targeted and bombed. Two months later, the home of the congregation's rabbi, Perry Nussbaum, was bombed while he and his wife slept, though both escaped serious injury. Like Atlanta's Rabbi Jacob Rothschild, Rabbi Nussbaum was an anti-segregation activist.

In 1977, the white supremacist Joseph Paul Franklin killed one worshipper and wounded two more in his attack on Congregation Brith Sholom Kneseth Israel in St. Louis.

In 1984, two members of The Order assassinated the popular radio talk show host Alan Berg in Denver. When asked why they'd chosen Berg, a founder of the group explained that he "was mainly thought to be anti-white and he was Jewish."

In 1999, the white supremacists Benjamin Matthew Williams and Tyler Williams—brothers—set three synagogues in Sacramento, California, on fire.

On April 28, 2000, the white supremacist Richard Baumhammers shot the windows of Congregation Beth El in my hometown of Pittsburgh and Congregation Ahavath Achim—the name translates to "brotherly love"— a bit more than five miles away in Carnegie, Pennsylvania. By the day's end, he had murdered Anil Thakur, Ji-ye Sun, Theo Pham, and Gary Lee and paralyzed Sandeep Patel—all racial minorities. Baumhammers began his rampage early in the afternoon when he invaded the home of his neighbor Anita Gordon, a Beth El congregant, shooting her dead and setting her house on fire. When the police searched his house, they found a manifesto for Baumhammers's so-called Free Market Party, which called for an end to nonwhite immigration.

There is nothing new about white supremacists targeting Jews. Our real fear, after Pittsburgh and Poway, was that America had somehow fundamentally changed.

The belief that America was capable of perfecting itself, or at least striving consistently toward that goal, was a secular article of American Jewish faith, the ontological justification for the sacrifices of our grandparents and their fierce attachment to a country whose greatness included the ability to improve, to shed parochial hatreds and become the beacon of freedom the founders had spoken of. We remembered and admired them, even with all of their own zealousness and blind spots and failures, because they had envisioned that possibility.

Our real fear now was that the once-marginal haters—the neo-Nazis, the white supremacists, the creeps and loons who celebrated mass killings from behind their iPhone screens—were no longer marginal. They had become the visible exemplars of a new political and cultural style that had overthrown long-standing sets of norms about tolerance, basic decency, and civility. The speech and behavior that had, until recently, been confined to basements and backrooms was now visible on Twitter and cable news. And the forty-fifth president was a huge fan of both.

. . .

Bigotry and anti-Semitism on the right long predated Donald Trump.

Traditionally, there were two kinds of anti-Semites in the GOP. The first were the genteel WASPs who, for a time, actually ran the Republican Party and whose influence stretched beyond Manhattan law firms and Connecticut country clubs to a State Department that was congenitally hostile to Israel. The second were Republicans from Catholic, working-class backgrounds whose animosity stemmed from a combination of isolationism, nativism, and pre–Vatican II Church doctrine.

In the early 1990s, one could see both. George H. W. Bush's secretary of state, James Baker, was an oil-business lawyer with close ties in the Persian Gulf who didn't have any personal affection for Jews or any professional liking for Israel. "Fuck the Jews," he allegedly said. "They don't vote for us anyway." Then there was Pat Buchanan. If anti-Semitism at the upper levels of the Republican Party was somewhat disguised, in figures like Buchanan, who mounted a primary challenge to Bush in 1992, one could find the movement's darkest tendencies. Like Lindbergh before him, he knew who was to blame for dragging America into Middle Eastern wars: "the Israeli Defense Ministry and its amen corner"—as in, American Jews. Capitol Hill, he said, was "Israel-occupied territory."

Buchanan's anti-Semitism might have been the one issue about which the *National Review*'s William F. Buckley and *The New York Times*'s Abe Rosenthal agreed. But the worst problem with Buchanan, as Charles Krauthammer observed in a March 1992 *Washington Post* column, "is not that his instincts are antisemitic but that they are, in various and distinct ways, fascistic." Buchanan attacked Bush as a "globalist" and insisted that the country needed a "new nationalism."

"This naked appeal to racial and ethnic exclusivity puts Buchanan firmly in the tradition of Jean-Marie Le

Pen and Europe's other neo-fascists whose platform is anti-immigrant resentment, fear and loathing of the unassimilated Other," Krauthammer wrote. Yet Buchanan would nonetheless be honored with the keynote address at the Republican National Convention that year. And he'd be alive to celebrate the victory of what his own campaign for president called "Make America First Again" when Donald Trump won the White House.

But whatever generalizations one wants to make about Republicans or the right—terms that today encompass a wide and disparate range of Americans, from secular libertarians to evangelicals to urban bankers to midwestern farmers to foreign-policy hawks to radical isolationists—there can be no question that recent Republican presidential candidates have been at pains to present themselves as men of faith who abhorred all forms of bigotry. No one ever accused President George W. Bush of schmoozing with anti-Semites. Just as the Bush family had seemingly changed or evolved, the Republican Party, like the rest of America, seemed to be changing and evolving.

Then came Trump. Casual racism had always been part of his life. Decades before he propagated the racist birther lie about President Barack Obama, Trump's real-estate company in New York City systemically discriminated against black applicants.

His views of Jews were more complex. On the one hand, his daughter and her husband are religiously observant Jews; in 2016, he boasted that Ivanka was "about to have a beautiful Jewish baby" during a speech to the American Israel Public Affairs Committee, or AIPAC, a pro-Israel lobbying group. To many, he appeared to be a philo-Semite, though as Deborah Lipstadt has sharply pointed out, a philo-Semite is merely "an anti-Semite who likes Jews." (As in: I got a new accountant. He's Jewish, so you know he'll get me a good deal.)

And yet before Charlottesville, and before his rant about immigrants from "shithole countries," Trump rode down that golden escalator in Trump Tower to tell voters that migrants from Mexico are "bringing drugs" and "bringing crime" and are "rapists." From the very start, Trump embodied a shameless and savage style of politics. He dismissed civility and decency as virtues for chumps, and cultivated a climate of rage and paranoia that has already proven deadly.

During Ronald Reagan's first presidential run, in 1980, he said of the KKK, which had come out in his support: "I have no tolerance with what the Klan represents and I want nothing to do with it." Four years later, when the hate group did the same, the president was even more adamant: "Those of us in public life can only resent the use of our names by those who seek political recognition for the repugnant doctrines of hate they espouse," he wrote in a May 1984 letter to the United States Commission on Civil Rights. "The politics of racial hatred and religious bigotry practiced by the Klan and others have no place in this country, and are destructive of the values for which America has always stood." By contrast, when

CNN's Jake Tapper asked Trump in February 2016 if he would "unequivocally condemn" David Duke's support and that of other white supremacists, Trump said, "Well, just so you understand, I don't know anything about David Duke, okay. I don't know anything about what you're even talking about with white supremacy or white supremacists. . . . I know nothing about David Duke, I know nothing about white supremacists."

It was a lie Trump himself exposed a week after the CNN interview, when he said on MSNBC's *Morning Joe:* "I disavowed him. I disavowed the KKK. Do you want me to do it again for the twelfth time?" Over time, will that lag between the lie of feigned ignorance and the grudging denunciation grow longer by him—or some other politician—who decides that there is more to be gained by refusing to ever capitulate or apologize?

· · ·

It is no accident that anti-Semites were drawn to Trump's banner: They recognized him as a fellow conspiracy theorist—and one willing to flirt with white supremacists. Trump played the major chords on which these bigots could riff for their followers.

Trump, like other populists around the world, had definitive answers for those Americans who felt left behind. The forces and the people keeping working men and women down, he said, were globalists, elitists, money, power, and special interests. What the Richard Spencers of the world—the neo-Nazis and white supremacists—heard was "Jew, Jew, Jew." Whether by design or because it reflected his inner gestalt, Trump gave them just enough reason to hear that word.

He still does.

"You're not going to support me because I don't want your money. You want to control your own politician, that's fine," he said to the Republican Jewish Coalition in 2015. At a speech in front of the same organization in 2019, Trump referred to Israeli Prime Minister Benjamin Netanyahu as "your prime minister," an obvious (if unwitting) accusation of Jewish dual loyalty. Of his former lawyer Michael Cohen, who cooperated with Robert Mueller's probe, he reportedly commented: "The Jews always flip."

When a man with this history says of the Unite the Right march in Charlottesville, "You also had some very fine people on both sides," white supremacists notice. When a man with this history says after fifty-one Muslims were murdered in Christchurch, New Zealand, by a white supremacist, "I think it's a small group of people that have very, very serious problems, I guess," the alt-right perks up at his minimization. Given the constant apologias that regularly issue forth from his minions—what he said after Charlottesville was "darn near perfection," declared the shameless Kellyanne Conway—is it any surprise that the far right sees an ally in this president and in the Republican Party, which Donald Trump has remade in his own image?

When the president of the party of Lincoln praises Robert E. Lee as a "great general," they hear the whistle. When the president talks not about patriotism but about nationalism, they hear the whistle. When he denigrates immigrants and declares "America first," they hear the whistle loud and clear.

Trump has never publicly praised the alt-right. But he doesn't have to. Statements like these are enough.

As was the presence of Steve Bannon, the president's political Rasputin, who made his political career by shaping and elevating the alt-right as a political force. First, he transformed Breitbart News into what he called "the platform for the 'alt-right'"—a safe space for digital taboo breakers, who happily advertised stories as "black crime." Then he leveraged it into a vehicle to elect Trump and to transform the GOP into a blunt-force instrument that actively portrayed liberal Jewish bankers and financiers as the hidden manipulators of American life.

Whereas the late William F. Buckley, as editor of *National Review,* cleansed what was then the country's most important conservative publication of anti-Semites, in part by firing one of his prominent editors, Joe Sobran, after he fell ill with the Jew-hating disease, Bannon's Breitbart happily played with fire. "Hell hath no fury like a Polish, Jewish, American elitist scorned," the website wrote of the journalist and historian Anne Applebaum. Bill Kristol, the anti-Trump conservative writer, was dubbed a "renegade Jew" by Breitbart. George Soros was branded "the Puppet Master." The comments section was, no surprise, an open sewer of bigotry.

Then Steve Bannon was sitting down the hall from the Oval Office, and President Trump was pushing for a Muslim ban crafted by his chief strategist. History wasn't moving in a straight line. The pendulum was swinging back.

Eight months into Trump's presidency, Bannon was ousted from the White House and Trump has shown little further appetite for openly praising white supremacists. Pundits rarely talk about Breitbart articles, though they remain as tendentious as ever. Richard Spencer, who coined the term "alt-right," has declared that the alt-right "failed" because it didn't have staying power beyond the fringe of the party.

But I fear that the decline of the alt-right per se is actually the beginning of a movement both more diffuse and more mainstream. The movement's poisonous ideology no longer lives only on Breitbart or on Reddit boards visited by disaffected keyboard warriors. Turn on Fox and you can hear "experts" talking about the "Soros-occupied State Department." In July, Breitbart's White House correspondent was hired by the White House. Meanwhile, Bannon crisscrosses Europe, regularly meeting with men like Nigel Farage and Viktor Orbán, trying to stoke blood-and-soil movements in countries with a real history of such politics.

Whether you see Trump as a primary cause of America's increasingly stark and violent divisions or as a symptom or as some combination of both, he has, at every opportunity, turned the temperature up rather than down. And he has genuinely appeared to have relished his role as the fomenter of chaos and conflict.

In the end, Trump's incessant dog whistling is less significant than the larger charge of which he stands guilty: the systemic removal of what my colleague Bret Stephens has called "the moral guardrails that keep bigotry down." Trump has done this by denigrating both the most heroic and the weakest people in our culture, by stoking angry mobs, by showing contempt for the rule of law and disdain for the very best of American traditions. He genuinely appears to take pleasure in the frothing crowds screaming, "Lock her up!" about Hillary Clinton and, more recently, "Shoot 'em!" about immigrants crossing the southern border. The naïve hope that he would grow into the office of the presidency now seems like a sick joke. His entire persona is built on upending order by betraying our allies and embracing our enemies, by shunning expertise and flirting with the fever swamps, and by seeking to break the already strained bonds of our affection.

When a man who has no use for better angels is in charge of the free world, who's to say when or how the chaos stops?

. . .

The rambling manifesto of John Earnest, the San Diego killer, is a toxic soup of two thousand years of anti-Semitism. At times, he sounds a bit like Martin Luther, blaming the Jews for killing Christ. He makes reference to history's most famous blood libel—that of two-year-old Simon of Trent, whose disappearance and death was blamed on the Jewish community, some members of which "confessed" after sustained torture. There are paragraphs that read as if they were written by Joseph Goebbels: Earnest rants about "feminism" and "degenerate" art and blames the Jews for their "race mixing," for their "sexual perversion," and for "peddling pornography." And there are the more modern canards: The Jews start wars. The Jews are guilty of "lying and deceiving the public through their exorbitant role in the news media." They control "all finances for the purpose of funding evil."

The killer also subscribes to what's called the Great Replacement theory, an old idea repackaged by a far-right French philosopher named Renaud Camus in his 2012 book *Le Grand Remplacement* and now in vogue on the far right in America and throughout Europe. "The great replacement is very simple," Camus has said. "You have one people, and in the space of a generation you have a different people."

This is the ideology behind a statement like this one tweeted and then repeated on television by Steve King, Republican congressman from Iowa: "We can't restore our civilization with somebody else's babies." "The Great

Replacement" was the name of the Christchurch killer's seventy-three-page manifesto.

Of course, the solution to this problem of "replacement" will be the same one anti-Semites have always reached for: Kill the Jews. But in each era, new conspiracies must be conjured, new justifications summoned. Thus the unique role the Jews play in replacement ideology, one I became aware of only after the Unite the Right rally in August 2017.

That event was a shattering awakening for those who believed that the poisonous ideology of white supremacy was mostly confined to the lunatic online fringe. That day, it turned out a crowd. Five hundred people showed up at the University of Virginia carrying tiki torches and enacted real violence in the offline world of flesh and blood. Two dozen innocent protestors were injured and one woman, thirty-two-year-old Heather Heyer, was murdered when a twenty-year-old white supremacist named James Alex Fields, Jr., plowed his Dodge Challenger into a group of people who had come to protest his ilk.

The supremacists marched across campus shouting the things you might expect: "Blood and soil," the English translation of the Nazi slogan *"Blut und Boden,"* and "White Lives Matter." But they also chanted a slogan I had never heard before: "Jews will not replace us."

At first I heard the line as maybe you did: We won't allow Jews to take our place—in college, in the corner office, wherever. It seemed straightforward. But I wasn't thinking enough like an anti-Semite. Behind the slogan "Jews will not replace us" is the ancient anti-Semitic notion of the Jew as the evil puppeteer, the devil behind the curtain pulling the strings. In this case, they are pulling them on behalf of black and brown people. How? By controlling progressive politicians, by organizing caravans of illegal immigrants to storm the southern border, and so on. This is certainly what Earnest believed—"I would die a thousand times over to prevent the doomed fate that the Jews have planned for my race"—and it is at the heart of the right-wing anti-Semitic conspiracy.

The "logic" goes like this: Whites are at the top. Blacks and browns and immigrants are at the bottom. And Jews occupy the duplicitous middle position. They can—and often do—appear to be white. But they are, in fact, slavishly loyal to those at the bottom. Thus the Jews are the ultimate betrayers of the white race, the most powerful racial enemy white people have.

This is why Erik K. Ward, a longtime anti-racist activist and the executive director of the Western States Center, has argued that anti-Semitism is only rightly understood as the "lynchpin of the White nationalist belief system." As he writes powerfully in his essay "Skin in the Game: How Antisemitism Animates White Nationalism," Jews, "despite and indeed because of the fact that they often read as White," are, in the view of white supremacists, "a different, unassimilable, enemy race that must be exposed, defeated, and ultimately eliminated."

That is just what Robbie Kaplan, the lawyer who is

suing the neo-Nazis who marched in Charlottesville, has said. These people "hate all of us—black, Muslim, LGBTQ people, women, immigrants. But the group they hate with the fiercest passion—the people they say they want to burn once again in ovens—are Jews."

As Ward notes, "At the bedrock of the movement is an explicit claim that Jews are a race of their own, and that their ostensible position as White folks in the U.S. represents the greatest trick the devil ever played." The Jews are the ultimate enemy of whites because they are the ones preventing whites' natural dominance.

We will see a mirror image of this ideology on the far left, among those who insist on tagging Jews as "white" as a way to strip them of their ability to claim victimhood, and who indulge their own kind of replacement theory, this one a version that relies on the lie of Jews having no indigenous connection to the land of Israel. This is the double bind in which American Jews are caught: They are at once white and nonwhite; the handmaidens of white supremacy and the handmaidens of immigrants and people of color; in league with the oppressed and in league with the oppressor.

. . .

There's a reason why Jewish Americans frequently reference the neo-Nazis marching in Skokie in 1977. It's less because it's a classic free-speech case and more that neo-Nazis don't march through the streets of American towns on most days. Social norms prevent this sort of thing from happening.

Only there is no shame on the Internet, no neighbor watching to cast a sideways glance. Here the alienated can connect with one another to form a common cause, even if their tattered social fabric is made of ones and zeros. You no longer have to meet a KKK grand wizard or an ISIS leader to be swept up in their cause. Self-radicalization is not only possible, but more and more common if you are a lonely soul already teetering on the edge.

A cottage industry of columnists has created an entire taxonomy of the Internet activity of the far right. After a bigot attacks a church or a mosque or a synagogue, these folks analyze each aspect of the attacker's online persona and behavior. Look! He never owned a copy of *Mein Kampf,* though he did post a meme of Pepe the Frog with a Hitler mustache. Look! Hours before he went into the synagogue, John Earnest posted his four-thousand-word screed to 8chan, where other users urged him to "get a high score"—gaming language to encourage him to kill as many people as possible.

The benefit to the reporter is clear: It seems like she knows about a secret world inaccessible to the average reader. But this pseudo-sophisticated process of decoding makes the subject seem almost mystical, when it is the opposite. A cartoon swastika on 8chan is still a swastika. The racism and anti-Semitism expressed on the Internet via meme is not some special new kind of racism and anti-Semitism. The hatred is the same as ever.

What is different, what the Internet does change, is the ability of these angry, hateful people to find community, and for interested parties—facilitators, ideologues, perverts, manipulators—to help them acquire the mental, emotional, and physical tools required to kill people.

To disguise this activity, the alt-right and its followers have used humor, sharply and effectively, as a way to deflect and avoid any responsibility. They flood the Web with "ironic" creations like "Shlomo Shekelberg," a caricature of a conniving, hook-nosed Jew straight out of *Der Stürmer*, and "Remove Kebab," a video that began its ill-fated Internet journey in Serbia as a piece of anti-Muslim propaganda and is now shorthand for the ethnic cleansing of Muslims throughout the West. When the obvious bigotry of such creations is called out, they say it's all a joke, just a bit of merry meme-making. Lighten up, guys like Milo Yiannopoulos say. It's the same all-in-good-fun defense offered up by notorious French comedian Dieudonné M'bala M'bala, who invented the anti-Semitic gesture known as the *quenelle*, defended it all as a hilarious joke, and then appeared on stage with Holocaust deniers like Robert Faurisson and Mahmoud Ahmadinejad. Ha.

This lame justification reminds me of an insight from Jean-Paul Sartre: "Never believe that anti-Semites are completely unaware of the absurdity of their replies.

They know that their remarks are frivolous, open to challenge. But they are amusing themselves, for it is their adversary who is obliged to use words responsibly, since he believes in words. The anti-Semites have the right to play. They even like to play with discourse for, by giving ridiculous reasons, they discredit the seriousness of their interlocutors. They delight in acting in bad faith, since they seek not to persuade by sound argument but to intimidate and disconcert."

When you are a Jewish journalist like Julia Ioffe or Ben Shapiro and your face is photoshopped into a gas chamber and people are threatening to murder you and your family, it's hard to LOL. I, too, have been a sometime target of these "ironists" and "satirists." My former editor at *Tablet*, Alana Newhouse, once bought me a necklace that read, "Comments Cause Cancer" after I received a particularly bruising pummeling by pixel. I consider it a serious prescription to never, ever click on the comment section. But I made an exception in January 2019, after I went on Joe Rogan's popular podcast.

I had breakfast a couple of days after the show with a friend who'd previously been on Rogan's podcast. He was worried that "something went wrong" for me. He was concerned that I was getting far more down votes than likes, and that there were lots of negative comments on the video, which was already well on its way to a million views on YouTube.

I chalked it up to a minor gaffe toward the end of the podcast when I criticized presidential hopeful Tulsi Gabbard, a woman suspiciously uncritical of Russia who, more suspiciously, hid from her party leadership that she had traveled to Syria as a Democratic congresswoman, where she met with Bashar al-Assad. I called Gabbard an Assad toady without bringing enough information to back up my claim. (Weeks later, she insisted that "Assad is not the enemy of the United States" on *Morning Joe,* leaving the chatty MSNBC panel temporarily speechless. But fair enough. It wasn't my strongest moment.)

When I looked at the online comments, however, I found that what had "gone wrong" was that I was a Jewish woman. Specifically, that I was a Jewish woman who had the gall to express her views in public, including my view that Israel is routinely demonized by those who claim to be mere critics of the state but are, in fact, anti-Semites.

The cancer was there in the open for anyone who decided to look at the comments beneath the video.

"Thanks Joe, for having this rootless cosmopolitan, this globalist, this swindler, on your show." There I was, like Soros, the internationalist loyal to no nation. Others suggested violence: "One of the worst human being still alive today. You know what should happen to that parasite."

More than one person posted a quote wrongly attributed to Voltaire: "If you want to know who rules over you, look at who you are not allowed to criticize," a variation on a line actually written by the American white nationalist and Holocaust denier Kevin Strom. (The actor

John Cusack made headlines in June when he tweeted this quote along with a caricature of a giant hand, adorned with a Jewish star, squashing a group of tiny people beneath it. His defense was priceless: "I didn't think 'Jews"when i saw it . . . all I thought was 'Israel.' ")

In many of the Rogan comments, three parentheses appeared around my name or around the whole of a comment. As in: "Joe and (((Bari))) are both cancer." The triple parentheses are by now an old enough meme that they have been reclaimed, with cheeky pride, by Jews on-line. But the echo, as it's often called, was originally used online to indicate someone's Jewishness without spelling it out. In many of the comments about me, the parentheses seemed redundant, given the explicit anti-Semitism of the words:

(((Rubs hands together greedily)))

Or:

(((Hears coins hit the ground, runs to pick them up)))

And:

(((why always them)))

While some of the comments could have been uttered by a Nazi in the 1940s—"Communist anti-white Jew"—others were unsuccessfully camouflaged in criticism of Israel that slid inexorably into diatribes about the Roths-childs, such as this gem: "More Americans are killed in a month by illegal aliens than Isrealis [*sic*] by Palestinians in a year. Yet, we send Isreal almost 4 billion a year to pay for their huge wall and border security and can't even put up a chain link fence along our border. In 2,001 there were 8 countries without a Rothschild owned central bank and now there are only 4 left. We have spent trillions in dollars and thousands of American lives just to give Jacob Rothschild more debt slaves."

As one commentator put it accurately: "Here's a complete comment section of Goyim knowing"—da goyim know, another meme implying a worldwide Jewish conspiracy. He deemed the phenomenon "beautiful." Months later, these people troll me relentlessly, asking me if I am related to Toucan Sam. Apparently our noses look similar.

· · ·

For some anti-Semites on the far right, Zionism—not as it actually exists, but as a twisted version of their own ethnonationalist fantasy—becomes the ultimate fig leaf. They insist that, as full-throated defenders of Israel, they are more pro-Israel than even most American Jews. So how can they possibly be anti-Semitic?

But if Jews by and large support and admire Israel because it aims to be an exponent of liberal democracy in the Middle East, because it is the fulfillment of a biblical promise, and because two thousand years of history have shown definitively that the Jewish people require a safe haven and an army, right-wing anti-Semites "love" Israel for the same reason they despise immigrants: Israel solves the problem of the Jews in their midst. It helps that they imagine Israel as a kind of anti-Muslim Sparta, not a democracy with a sizable (nearly 20 percent) Muslim minority. "You could say that I am a white Zionist—in the sense that I care about my people, I want us to have a secure homeland for us and ourselves," Richard Spencer said in 2017 on Israeli Channel 2.

Yair Rosenberg has summed up this twisted and disingenuous move concisely in *Tablet*. "The alt-right maliciously appropriates the deeply held values of liberals and minorities in order to attack them," he wrote. "In this manner, the return of Jews to their indigenous homeland is recast by white nationalists, who are not indigenous to America, to justify kicking Jews and other minorities out of the country."

The tragedy is that the Netanyahu government has increasingly made the alt-right's claim that much easier, by aligning the Jewish state with the right-wing governments of countries like Hungary and Poland, whose current leaders are outspoken defenders of Israel even as they stoke bigotry and Holocaust revisionism at home.

The Israeli government's logic goes like this: Israel stands alone in a hostile world and in an especially violent neighborhood. It needs whatever friends it can get. As far as Bibi's government is concerned, as a senior Israeli official put it to me, the ideology of Viktor Orbán is far less of a threat to world Jewry than the ideology of Jeremy Corbyn. Thus we witness breathtaking spectacles like Rodrigo Duterte of the Philippines, a man who has compared himself to Hitler, being treated with honor at Yad Vashem, Israel's Holocaust museum.

I realize that all nations engage in realpolitik, and that in making such alliances Israel is proving that it is nothing other than a normal country. But the embrace of these authoritarians, at least right now, by the Israeli government is deeply painful for anyone who, like me, believes that a Jewish state should be imbued with Jewish values. Thankfully that includes Israel's current president, Reuven Rivlin, who has remarked, "You cannot say 'We admire Israel and want relations with your country, but we are neo-fascists.' Neo-fascism is absolutely incompatible with the principles and values on which the State of Israel was founded."

. . .

Those who thought the election of Donald Trump was simply an overreaction to the progressive presidency of Barack Obama suffered from a profound failure of imagination. Donald Trump is a small symptom of a trend sweeping the globe. People everywhere are turning away from internationalism and toward isolationism, away from globalization and toward nationalism, away from open borders and toward closed ones. Nowhere is this wave more visible than in Europe, where people, especially young people, are warming to authoritarianism and turning their backs on liberal democracy.

No one has diagnosed this movement better than the historian and *Washington Post* columnist Anne Applebaum and the political scientist Yascha Mounk (*The People vs. Democracy*). Both have powerfully demonstrated how and why the demonization of minorities and Jews is less than a hop, skip, and a jump away from these populists' main claims.

All of these parties and figures begin by seizing on real challenges faced by their countries. They harp on dramatic demographic changes, whether the result of refugees, economic migration, or simply birth rates. They highlight persistent economic stagnation for the middle and working classes, which is the inevitable result of automation and globalization. They say that the vast majority of wealth remains in the hands of a vanishing few and that people feel unmoored and alone because of the lack of a coherent common culture, the weakening of religion, and the disintegration of cultural institutions.

Responsible politicians operating in healthy societies would talk soberly about these challenges and offer policies and compromises to address them. But the leaders in this autocratic mold instead exploit, exaggerate, and demonize, while often suggesting cruel and crude solutions to these complicated problems. Trump's Muslim ban comes immediately to mind.

In the meantime, and in the absence of healthy centrism, many progressive politicians practice avoidance. They ignore real social tensions associated with mass immigration, unsure about how to acknowledge those tensions without stoking xenophobia, alienating their perceived base, or being smeared as bigots. They downplay patriotism, afraid of stoking jingoism or of being accused of it. They ignore the need for a return to a common culture or even a set of civic values, lest they be accused of promoting cultural intolerance.

It's difficult to overstate the severity of this error. It has meant that progressives have abandoned the political field to those on the very far right, as journalists like David Frum and James Kirchick and scholars like Karen Stenner (*The Authoritarian Dynamic*) and Eric Kaufmann (*Whiteshift*) have all pointed out. In the absence of serious liberal answers to these significant questions, the bluntness of authoritarian populists becomes that much more seductive to the average voter, who comes to see liberals as evasive and out of touch. Especially because what these populists promise is straightforward: They will prioritize the needs of their country's "real" citizens. They'll return their country to those to whom it really belongs. They promise to look inward; to stop adventures abroad; to put "America first."

For the disaffected and the frustrated and the left behind, it is a message whose appeal cannot be underestimated. This is the reason we need a healthy version of patriotism, a healthy version of American pride, and a healthy conversation about hard topics like immigration. It is necessary both for the future of liberal democracy and for the sake of the Jews, who serve as the perfect scapegoat for these populist nationalists.

At this point, I can feel my conservative and Trump-curious readers rolling their eyes. They insist that the anti-Semitism of the alt-right, unlike the anti-Semitism of the British Labour Party, which is coordinated and voiced by those at the very top, is a body with no head. In this, they seem to have the backing of Christopher Wray, the FBI director, who has said that right-wing, white supremacist violence tends to be "less organized" and carried out by "one-off individuals as opposed to some structured hierarchy."

They point out that while both houses of Congress voted to move the embassy to Jerusalem, only Trump, with his total disregard for the niceties of diplomatic hypocrisy, acted on what was, after all, the will of the American people through their democratically elected representatives. Only Trump was willing to recognize Israeli sovereignty over the Golan Heights, leaving no possibility that it will ever return to the bloody hands of Assad.

So, okay, they'll admit: Trump is disgusting. He has said horrible things about minorities. He's even said anti-Semitic things. And yet Trump has also condemned anti-Semitism in unequivocal terms, which cannot be said of many in the Democratic Party. In his State of the Union address in February 2019 he said of Iran: "We will not avert our eyes from a regime that chants 'Death to America' and threatens genocide against the Jewish people. We must never ignore the vile poison of anti-Semitism, or those who spread its venomous creed. With one voice, we must confront this hatred anywhere and everywhere it occurs." After Pittsburgh, he issued a full-throated condemnation of the act, which revealed an understanding of anti-Semitism: "This wicked act of mass murder is pure evil, hard to believe, and, frankly, something that is unimaginable," he said. "Anti-Semitism and the widespread persecution of Jews represents one of the ugliest and darkest features of human history. The vile, hate-filled poison of anti-Semitism must be condemned and confronted everywhere and anywhere it appears." Whatever one thinks of Trump, the statement was strong. And yet a *New Yorker* writer devoted an entire critical piece to his use of the word "frankly" in that first sentence—which only served as further evidence among Trump-supporting Jews that the president's virtues vis-à-vis the Jewish community were getting overlooked.

Finally, they point out that many of these extremists, including the Pittsburgh and Poway killers, despise Donald Trump. They accuse him, variously, of being in bed with the Jews, of being a globalist, of giving his daughter away to a Jew, and of being controlled by the Jewish lobby or the ZOG, the Zionist-occupied government.

But all of this overlooks the terrible truth, which is that in the nearly three years he has been in office, Donald Trump has trashed—gleefully and shamelessly—the unwritten rules of our society that have kept American Jews and, therefore, America safe. The harm in this cannot be overstated. Policies, good or bad, can be undone. Politicians can be voted out. But a culture demolished, smashed, twisted beyond recognition? That is much harder to repair.

. . .

There are two comforts, if it's possible to say such a thing, when it comes to right-wing anti-Semitism. The first is that it does not hide its face. It is blunt in its goals. The second is that in fighting neo-Nazis, Jews are aligned with our natural political allies: liberals. When the far right attacks us, we find sympathy and support from progressives, who tend to be overwhelmingly represented in our neighborhoods and workplaces. We are the right kind of victims with the right kind of enemies.

But while white supremacists tend to be the most violent—there is a very high likelihood that if someone walks into your synagogue with a gun, that person will be a creature of the far right—they account for only a small percentage of anti-Semitic acts. There were 1,879 incidents of anti-Semitism in America in 2018, according to the Anti-Defamation League. Just 13 percent of them (249) were carried out by members of white supremacist groups. "What this suggests is that the rise of anti-Semitic incidents is not the result of a vast underground conspiracy and widespread recruitment by white nationalist groups," ADL chief Jonathan Greenblatt told me. "What we're seeing is actually much worse. What we are seeing is the normalization of anti-Semitism. To express humor, to express frustration, to express anxiety, to just let it out."

There are not a lot of white supremacists walking around New York City, which has the largest Jewish population of any city in the country. And yet in 2019, more than half (57 percent) of all hate crimes in New York targeted Jews, according to the NYPD. These are the kind of attacks that people like Avram Mlotek, a young rabbi who wears a kippah, has experienced repeatedly in the city. "The Jew is very fucking dangerous," a man yelled at him the other day in the 168th Street subway station in Washington Heights. "You are very dangerous. I want all the Jews out of Cuba and Palestine. The Jews are very dangerous!" Another time Mlotek was on the train and a man held up a picture of Louis Farrakhan. "That's a real Jew," he said. "You're a fucking fake."

Alas for the Jews, we don't get to choose who hates us.

CHAPTER 4

THE LEFT

I s the anti-Semitism that posits that Jews are evil capitalists who control the world different from the one that
posits that they are evil communists who control the
world? Is the anti-Semitism that insists that Jews connive
and exploit gentile power different from the one that insists that they connive and exploit via their own state
power? Is the anti-Semitism that says that Jews are secret
betrayers of the white race different from the anti-
Semitism that says they are secret white supremacists? Is
the anti-Semitism that asserts Jews have upended tradition any different than the anti-Semitism that asserts
that they stand in the way of progress? Is the anti-
Semitism that forces us to designate ourselves publicly
with Jewish stars different from the anti-Semitism that
insists we must not?

One form of the hatred originates on the political
right, the other on the left. They may seem wildly differ-

ent at first glance, but they are mirror images of the same derangement. And each one reaches the same conclusion, though perhaps at slightly different speeds: Eliminate the Jew.

Yet American Jews tend to be much more attuned to anti-Semitism when it comes from the political right. Certainly this is a function of Hitler's long shadow. But it is also because American Jews have a deep affinity with the political left, and for sound reasons.

For those fleeing the oppressions of Eastern Europe, the only natural home was the party of the underdog, the immigrant, and the outsider. Ashkenazi Jews who moved to America en masse beginning in the nineteenth century swiftly took their places in, and sometimes at the helms of, progressive movements. And though American Jews have attained the kind of financial success that typically translates into voting Republican, at least for the time being they continue to vote overwhelmingly for Democrats.

There is perhaps a deeper religious reason beyond the obvious political one for the Jewish alignment with the left. As Steven R. Weisman argues in his recent book *The Chosen Wars,* Jews in America created a new Judaism—one that largely untethered itself from a specific geography (the land of Israel) and a specific goal (the messianic age). In this new iteration, America became the promised land, and the notion of *tikkun olam,* repairing the world, took the place of the Messiah. The new goal of American Jews, especially non-Orthodox ones, was not to return to the Holy Land (after all, they were already in one) or to pray to God to usher in a messianic age. The new goal was to perfect their new Israel. They would be the implements of this country's messianic age—saving America would come not from the heavens but from American Jews themselves.

The problem with this assumed accord between liberal politics and Jews is that it blinds us into thinking that anti-Semitism is only a problem of the right, a fantasy that falls apart under the gentlest scrutiny. Just as there is modern anti-Semitism that traces back to Hitler, there is also modern anti-Semitism that begins with Lenin and intensifies with Stalin.

Hitlerian anti-Semitism announces its intentions unequivocally. But leftist anti-Semitism, like communism itself, pretends to be the opposite of what it actually is.

Because of the easy way it can be smuggled into the mainstream and manipulate us—who doesn't seek justice and progress? who doesn't want a universal brotherhood of man?—anti-Semitism that originates on the political left is more insidious and perhaps more existentially dangerous. If you want to see the stakes, just look across the pond, where Jeremy Corbyn, an anti-Semite, has successfully transformed one of the country's great parties into a hub of Jew hatred.

Corbynism is not confined to the U.K. Right now in America, leftists who share Corbyn's worldview are building grassroots movements and establishing factions within the Democratic Party that are actively hostile to

Jewish power, to Israel, and, ultimately, to Jews. Those Jews who want to remain progressives in good standing within those groups are being asked to erase more and more of themselves to remain inside the fold.

Some don't even know they are making this choice, having grown up with little Jewish education or understanding of Jewish history. But others do. And they are doing so not because a regime, as in the Soviet Union, is forcing them to at pain of losing a good job or being subjected to forced labor or worse. They are making this choice of their own volition, desperate not to be frozen out of the communities they imagine are theirs, desperate to feel at home in the political movements to which they have given time and capital, desperate not to be alienated from the institutions they have helped build, and desperate not to lose their good names, which can happen in an instant in our digital age.

I meet such people in every Jewish community I speak to. They tend to wait until late in the evening, after the crowd has thinned out or after they've had a few glasses of wine, to make their confession. But the confession is always the same: I'm in the closet. It is not their sexuality or gender expression they are closeting. It is their Jewishness and their Zionism.

Why are these Jews in hiding? More specifically, why are they hiding in the progressive circles in which they live and work and protest and date and marry and parent, in the circles hyperobsessed with embracing authenticity, in the circles that promise preferred pronoun usage?

They are doing this because they understand that, increasingly, progressivism is asking them to make a choice. Are you one of the good guys or one of the bad guys? Do you side with the racists or their victims? Are you part of the coalition of the oppressed or the coalition of the oppressor?

In order to be welcomed as a Jew in a growing number of progressive groups, you have to disavow a list of things that grows longer every day. Whereas once it was enough to criticize Israeli government policy, specifically its treatment of Palestinians, now Israel's very existence must be denounced. Whereas once it was enough to forswear the Jewish Defense League, now the very idea of Jewish power must be abjured. Whereas once Jewish success had to be explained, now it has to be apologized for. Whereas once only Israel's government was demonized, now it is the Jewish movement for self-determination itself.

This bargain, which is really an ultimatum, explains so much.

It is why Jewish leaders of the Women's March were subjected to anti-Semitic attacks and exclusion by the movement's other leaders.

It is why at the University of Virginia, Jewish student activists were barred from admission in a minority student coalition to fight white supremacy.

It is why Michael Goldstein, a religiously observant and Zionist faculty member at Kingsborough Community College, in Brooklyn, has been the victim of a dehumanizing campaign. First "kill Zionist Entity" was scrawled on a photograph of his late father, a former president of the school. Then flyers were distributed on campus accusing Goldstein of bigotry. Some included pictures of his thirteen-year-old daughter. He now has full-time security.

It is why Manny's, a popular progressive café and event space in San Francisco, is being regularly protested. It's because its owner—a gay, progressive, Mizrahi Jew—is, according to the protestors, "a Zionist and a gentrifier."

It is why Jewish lesbians holding rainbow flags with Jewish stars were kicked out of the Dyke March in Chicago in 2017. And why, two years later, the Dyke March in Washington, D.C., officially banned flags with Jewish stars, under the guise of banning "nationalist symbols." It's an incredible admission of ignorance, considering that the Jewish star appeared on synagogues as early as the third century. And the idea that the Jewish star is merely a symbol of Jewish power is a breathtaking claim to anyone who has ever seen a picture of a Jew forced to wear a yellow one under the Nazis. The neo-Nazis who showed up at a pride celebration in Detroit the very same weekend as the Dyke March to urinate on an Israeli flag surely know that.

But more to the point: The antidote to the abuse heaped on the Jewish star of self-determination isn't the embrace of the yellow star the Nazis used to label their victims, even if doing so gets you a seat at certain tables. On the contrary, the Jewish star lives in all its fullness, ancient and modern, as fitting on the flag of the Jewish national home as it is marking the grave of an American Jewish soldier in Arlington.

As the journalist Batya Ungar-Sargon observed: "If there's only room in your movement for the 3% of Jews who say they aren't pro-Israel, your movement effectively bans Jews." No, no, the march organizers insisted, we are just banning the symbols of "nations that have specific oppressive tendencies." Which makes it all the more incredible that they were fine with Palestinian flags, given that gayness itself is deeply taboo in Palestinian society and can get you killed by groups like Hamas. (A 2014 Pew poll found that 1 percent of Palestinians felt that homosexuality is "morally acceptable.")

It is worthwhile to pause and consider the breathtaking twist of history here. Once anti-Semitism required Jews to publicly mark themselves. Now, in some of the precincts of progressivism, anti-Semitism requires them not to.

And just as those on the far right have an out when accused of anti-Semitism—we like Jews just fine so long as they self-deport to Israel and keep our country unsullied—those on the far left have an out as well. We like Jews just fine, they say, as long as they shed their stubborn particularism and adhere, without fail, to our ever-shifting ideas of justice and equality. Jews are welcome so long as they undertake a kind of secular conversion by disavowing many or most of the things that actually make them Jewish. Whereas Jews once had to convert to Christianity, now they have to convert to anti-Zionism.

These cases and hundreds of similar ones playing out across the country are surely part of what's motivating those who tell me that they are preemptively censoring themselves in liberal spaces—by taking off a kippah before walking into a college seminar; by pretending not to hear when someone suggests that Israel does not have a right to exist; by allowing a comment about "white Jews" to pass without correction; by standing by as other Jews, the "wrong kind," are denigrated and dehumanized.

Very few of these people fear literal violence. What these Jews dread is something more intimate and more likely: moral condemnation, social ostracism, and reputational vilification meted out by peers, professors, friends, and political allies. To be a good progressive increasingly requires distorting Jewish history and disavowing the Jewish state. Telling the truth is not worth the risk to reputations, careers, or social standing.

But because the violence here is usually not physical, many of my progressive readers and friends tell me that it is ridiculous to draw any kind of comparison or moral equivalence between white supremacy and what is coming out of the left, which they insist is basically criticism of Israel run amok. The "real" anti-Semites—the ones that shoot up synagogues—exist only on the right. To draw any attention away from that threat is not just irresponsible, they maintain, it is dangerous. As if hate were a zero-sum game.

How dare I use my platform, some say, on a phenomenon so much less urgent, a phenomenon that is certainly far less lethal? It leaves me wondering: When *can* we speak out about it?

It is, of course, true that left-wing professors, activists, tech workers, artists, lawyers, and doctors aren't the kind of Americans who tend to own automatic weapons. Nor will these people ever come out and say something so blunt as "Kill the Jews." No, anti-Semitism that originates on the left is a far more subtle and sophisticated enterprise. It's typically camouflaged in language familiar to Jewish tongues and ears: the language of social justice and anti-racism, of equality and liberation.

This anti-Semitism cloaks itself in the false guise of political difference—it claims to be "criticism of Israel" or "just anti-Zionism"—and demands that it be lauded for its noble goals: fighting racism, fighting nationalism, championing the downtrodden. This is how it successfully inoculates itself from criticism. Because in this perverse equation, anyone who points out that anti-Zionism is anti-Semitic, in effect if not in intent, is defending racism and nationalism. It puts me in mind of Susan Sontag's famous observation that communism is fascism with a human face.

And yet it remains hard for many to see it as threatening because it attempts, at least at first, only to marginalize Jews rather than to murder us.

Ben Hecht, one of the greatest screenwriters of his generation, wrote about this conundrum in a 1944 book called *A Guide for the Bedevilled*. Hecht describes receiving a letter in the mail from an anonymous person: "Across the page in large red crayon letters are scrawled the words, 'Kill All The Jews.'" He muses about who might have sent the letter. It was probably not the smartest of men, probably someone who delighted in imagining the fear Hecht would feel when he read it. But, Hecht notes, "not all anti-Semites write in red crayon. Many of them write in fine ink, Monsieur Voltaire, for instance. Monsieur Voltaire does not come in my mail. He stands on my bookshelf with all his electric sentences alive between covers."

The letter written in red crayon? The screenwriter easily tosses it into the garbage bin. Unfortunately, Voltaire, the prince of reason, is much harder to dismiss. "Monsieur Voltaire is open on my desk," Hecht writes. "He is much more articulate than my correspondent from Hollywood. He depresses me much more. Perhaps this is because I am more sensitive to crimes of the intellect than to those of the body. They are more dangerous—because they are more lasting."

Neo-Nazis, in a way, are easy. We know they wish us dead. Anti-Semites with PhDs, the ones who defend their bigotry as enlightened thinking, are harder to fight. And so American Jews are confronting two fears at the same time, one from without and one from within: Being shot by white supremacists. And being made out to be them.

. . .

In 2017, 58.1 percent of all religion-motivated hate crimes in the United States were carried out against Jews. (By contrast, 18.6 percent targeted Muslims.) If you mark each of these anti-Jewish crimes on a map of the United States, you will see that almost all of them occurred in predominantly blue states. That is where Jews tend to live. Including me.

I hang out in places that Sarah Palin would definitely not consider "real America." I like arugula. I work at the "failing" *New York Times.* For these reasons, while my online world is overrun with denizens of the alt-right, I don't often encounter people who call me a "slippery Jewess" in the real world.

Yet I've had a front row seat to leftist anti-Semitism. Indeed, I have been watching it grow in power since I was a student at Columbia University, a place where I was taught in many classes, in the dining halls, and in campus bars that you couldn't be both a progressive in good standing and a Zionist.

During my sophomore year, I took a lecture course on the history of the Middle East. One day, on a subway ride downtown, I ran into a classmate from the course who I'd met in a literature seminar the year before. We were friendly. She confessed that she had a question. You're a reasonable liberal, she said. So how can you be a Zionist? How can you support a racist ideology?

This student was in no way an anti-Semite. She was a

California WASP who had known little about the region before enrolling in this introductory course. It was being taught by a then-untenured professor named Joseph Massad, a man who had declared that "The Jews are not a nation" and "The Jewish state is a racist state that does not have a right to exist." Massad made clear that one of the ideological planks of being a good progressive was to be an anti-Zionist. To believe that a state that accounts for less than 1 percent of the land mass of the Middle East is at the root of that region's problems. To believe that one flawed state of all the flawed states in the world—a world including Syria and North Korea and China and Russia—did not deserve to fix its flaws but had to be wiped off the map.

By the time I got to college, in 2003, this view of Israel—not as the culmination of two thousand years of Jewish yearning, or as the repatriation of an indigenous people, or even as a safe haven for the Jewish people, but as the last bastion of white colonialism in the Middle East—had conquered departments across campus that had embraced postmodern, postcolonial theory. Nowhere, however, was the demonization of Israel and of Israeli Jews more aggressively pursued than in the school's Middle Eastern studies department.

In 2004, Hamid Dabashi, then the head of the Middle Eastern studies department, wrote a piece for the Egyptian *Al-Ahram Weekly*. "Half a century of systematic maiming and murdering of another people has left its deep marks on the faces of these people," he wrote of Israeli Jews. "The way they talk, the way they walk, the way they handle objects, the way they greet each other, the way they look at the world. There is an endemic prevarication to this machinery, a vulgarity of character that is bone-deep and structural to the skeletal vertebrae of its culture." Dabashi has referred to Zionists as "master thieves" and "laughing hyaenas" [*sic*]. In May 2018 he posted on Facebook: "Every dirty treacherous ugly and pernicious happening in the world just wait for a few days and the ugly name of 'Israel' will pup" [*sic*].

A decade ago, the situation at Columbia seemed like it was exceptional. A few years ago, there would be one anti-Zionist scandal on a college campus each year or maybe each semester. Now there are several each week. And the lived experience of committed Jews and Zionists on campus has gotten much, much uglier.

Take NYU as an example. The school has all of the qualities that would seem to make it an ideal place for Jewish students: There is a big Jewish community (some 13 percent of undergraduates), a thriving Hillel, and it is located in the heart of New York City, which boasts the largest Jewish population of any metropolis in the world. Yet it is there that Doria Kahn, a rising junior, has been told that she must have a lot of money, that her people "control" New York, and that it's an exaggeration to state that six million Jews were killed in the Holocaust. She has heard her fellow students say that Jews have nothing to complain about because they are the most privileged group in America. "None of those comments have been from alt-right neo-Nazis," she says. "They have come from my teachers and supposed friends."

The broader political landscape at NYU suggests why Kahn is being treated this way. In December 2018, the student government successfully passed a BDS resolution—joining the movement to boycott Israel that is opposed to any Jewish state between the Jordan River and the Mediterranean Sea—calling on the school to divest from any firms that do business with Israel. A few months later, the school's Department of Social and Cultural Analysis decided to boycott the university's study abroad program in Israel, an especially notable development considering its lack of a boycott of the United Arab Emirates—a country where NYU has an affiliated school and where there is modern slavery. Then NYU gave the President's Service Award, the school's highest honor, to Students for Justice in Palestine. To cap off the year, writer Steven Thrasher used the occasion of his graduation speech at the Graduate School of Arts & Science to say: "I am so proud, so proud, of NYU's chapters of Students for Justice in Palestine and of Jewish Voice for Peace . . . for supporting the Boycott, Divestment, and Sanctions movement against the apartheid state government in Israel because this is what we are called to do."

In the days that followed, various publications dug up incendiary tweets from Thrasher, and the school's president, Andrew Hamilton, apologized, saying he was "shocked" by "these undoubtedly vile and anti-Semitic tweets." But it was too little, too late.

Thrasher is now a professor at Northwestern's Medill School of Journalism. UCLA professor Judea Pearl, the father of the late *Wall Street Journal* journalist Daniel Pearl, is an NYU graduate who returned his distinguished alumnus award after his alma mater gave an award to Students for Justice in Palestine. He said this of the school's choice of commencement speaker: "Thrasher demonstrates that, when soil conditions are right, poisonous weeds can grow in our best universities, on our own very watch. I dread the thought that a racist deformity of such toxicity will be given a podium and clone students at Northwestern University. The public trusts us, educators, with the soil conditions; are we worthy of the trust?"

Ellen Schanzer, an incoming freshman, decided the answer was no. Schanzer's great-grandfather Martin Bernstein had once been chairman of the school's Music Department, yet Schanzer came to the conclusion that if she were to matriculate at NYU, she "would be," she wrote, "affiliating myself with an institution that accommodates faculty members and student organizations that are dedicated to anti-Semitic ideologies." Her letter to the school continued: "Some on your campus differentiate between anti-Zionism and anti-Semitism; however, I am not one of those people. This age-old hatred of my people wears different disguises in different generations, but [its] root objective is always the same."

If trends at American universities continue apace, I suspect that committed Jews will follow Schanzer's lead and avoid campuses where, as she put it in her letter, their "core beliefs and very existence is being threatened." Indeed, the word "Zionist" itself has become a casual slur at many schools. During my sister's freshman orientation at the University of Michigan, for instance, she overheard two young women on the quad talking about a guy one of them was hooking up with. Everything about him seemed great. The deal breaker: "I can't date a Zionist." Four years later, Michigan's student government passed BDS.

Classical anti-Semitic incidents (swastika graffiti, say, which appeared at least twice in 2018 at Duke) still outnumber anti-Zionist incidents on college campuses, according to Amcha, an organization that tracks anti-Semitism on campuses in the United States. But the numbers belie two important differences between the two types. First, in "classical" anti-Semitic cases, the perpetrator typically acts alone and without any organizational affiliation. Second, in the vast majority of anti-Zionist incidents, the perpetrator was "intent on harming pro-Israel members of the campus community" and was seven times more likely to be affiliated with groups than classic cases. According to Amcha's 2017 campus report, "Israel-related incidents were significantly more likely to contribute to a hostile campus."

The goal, even if unspoken, of these activists and professors is to make their schools hostile to certain core Jewish ideas, and thus to Jews who hold them dear. As Einat Wilf, a former Labor member of Knesset, has put it,

"Antisemitism works by increasingly restricting spaces where Jews can feel welcome and comfortable, until none are left."

The problem is not only that on the vast majority of elite campuses anti-Zionism has now become a plank of progressivism, alongside abortion rights, drug legalization, and racial justice. It's also that these trends have leapt far beyond the quad and into the real world, where Israel's right to exist is now being challenged—either implicitly or explicitly—by people with tremendous political and cultural power, including celebrated intellectuals like Michelle Alexander, author of *The New Jim Crow*, and buzzed-about Democratic members of Congress like Michigan's Rashida Tlaib.

BDS may not have succeeded in passing on many campuses, but it has very much succeeded in shaping the worldview of progressives, more and more of whom have come to believe that Israel is on the wrong side of history, that to identify as a Zionist is to identify as a racist, and that—most breathtaking of all—the Jewish state itself is a white supremacist project.

When anti-Zionism becomes a normative political position, active anti-Semitism becomes the norm. Because if you believe that Zionism is racism, it follows that Zionists are racists. And everyone knows what should happen to racists.

· · ·

Is it fair to equate anti-Zionism with anti-Semitism?

The former chief rabbi of the United Kingdom, Rabbi Jonathan Sacks, has put it plainly: "In the Middle Ages Jews were hated for their religion. In the nineteenth and early twentieth century, they were hated for their race. Today they are hated for their nation state, Israel." All three types of hate insist on the same thing: "Jews have no right to exist collectively as Jews with the same rights as other human beings."

And yet it's easy to make the intellectual case that anti-Zionism and anti-Semitism are distinct.

First, there is a long history of anti-Zionist Jews. Anti-Zionist Jews today point most readily (and proudly) to the Bund, which emerged in Russia in 1897, the same year that Theodor Herzl formed the World Zionist Organization. Herzl's solution to the Jewish plight was Jewish self-determination. The socialists of the Bund begged to differ. The way to address Europe's rampant anti-Semitism was not running away to the Middle East, the Bund argued, but staying put and joining together with the working class in solidarity.

The Bund and the world they defended no longer exists. Yet their ideas—ideas that, unlike Zionism, were not able to save Jews from systemic oppression or mass murder—are today being taken up once again. The crucial difference, of course, is that when the Bund opposed Israel in early-twentieth-century Russia, the state did not actually exist. Nor did the group know of the bloodletting that Hitler would unleash on Europe. And yet despite the lessons of history, various left-wing groups, some primarily populated by Jews, continue to oppose the existence of the Jewish state.

Some Jews have long and ardently opposed the creation of a Jewish state on theological grounds. They believe that until the Messiah comes, the Jews have no business establishing a state in the Holy Land. This is the view of groups such as Neturei Karta, a group as marginal to twenty-first-century Judaism as the Westboro Baptist Church is to Christianity. Yet its members are held up as Jews par excellence by left-wing anti-Semites like Jeremy Corbyn, as well as by right-wing governments like the Islamic Republic of Iran. One member of Neturei Karta even worked under Yasser Arafat: Moshe Hirsch was his minister of Jewish affairs.

There is also a history of anti-Semitic Zionists. Arthur Balfour was the British foreign secretary who made a Jewish return to the land of Israel official British policy. In 1917, he wrote a short letter to Lord Rothschild stating, "His Majesty's Government view with favour the establishment in Palestine of a national home for the Jewish people, and will use their best endeavours to facilitate the achievement of this object, it being clearly understood that nothing shall be done which may prejudice the civil and religious rights of existing non-Jewish communities in Palestine, or the rights and political status enjoyed by Jews in any other country."

But the author of the famous Balfour Declaration also supported Jewish immigration to the land of Israel because he didn't want Eastern European Jews fleeing pogroms to come to his country. That was why he had supported a 1905 law limiting their immigration to England. The Polish government supported immigration of its Jews to Israel in the 1930s for the same anti-Semitic reasons.

Today there remain some anti-Zionist Jews, just as there are some Zionist anti-Semites. But pointing to these fringe ideologies—and they are quite fringe; the vast majority of Jews in the world identify as Zionists—fails to address the current reality that Israel exists. It is not an abstraction.

So when people say they are anti-Zionist, it is important to be clear about what they seek. What they seek is the elimination of an actual state in the Jewish ancestral home where more than six million Jews, more than half of whom have roots in the Middle East, live with their families, not to mention some two million non-Jewish citizens, who are not spared when Israel is attacked by its enemies. With the notable exception of a few hundred committed anarchists in Brooklyn and Berkeley who think all nation-states should disappear, anti-Zionists do not support the elimination of any other country in the world. Just one state. The Jewish one.

Many of us have largely become numb to the reality that there is a significant political movement in the West that believes only one state in the world is illegitimate. Why just this one state, given that so many other modern states (Lebanon, Iraq, Syria) were likewise forged in war and displacement, their borders drawn by imperial powers whose empires have faded. Why is just this one illegitimate?

And what happens when the anti-Zionist dream—a one-state solution or the elimination of Israel—is imposed? To have even the most superficial understanding of Middle Eastern politics and history is to know that it would result in massive carnage or genocide less than seventy-five years after the end of the Holocaust. If the Christian experience in the region—not to mention that of the Yazidis or the Zoroastrians—has taught us anything, it is that minorities in the contemporary Middle East cannot survive without protection. When anti-Zionists think about what would happen were their vision to be fulfilled, do they imagine that Israelis would pack their bags and head back to Afghanistan and Hungary and Ethiopia? Of course not. They would fight. The kumbaya of the anti-Zionist dream guarantees a very bloody reality, and anti-Zionists should be forced to defend it.

Anti-Zionists regularly claim that they are just criticizing Israel, and that those who call them out as anti-Semites are simply trying to silence that criticism. British scholar David Hirsh dubbed this the Livingstone Formulation, after the former London mayor Ken Livingstone, who went on an anti-Semitic tear in 2005 and insisted that those outraged by his obvious anti-Semitism were just trying to shut up his criticism of Israel. The Livingstone Formulation, Hirsh has written, "is a means of refusing to engage with an accusation of antisemitism; instead it reflects back an indignant counter-accusation, that the accuser is taking part in a conspiracy to silence political speech." The device allows the accused both to smear the person bringing the charge with bad faith and also to conflate even overt anti-Semitism as fair criticism of Israel.

It is doubtless the case that legitimate criticism of Israel is sometimes misheard as something darker. But often, despite anti-Zionists' claims, it works in the opposite way. At a festival in Oslo this March, for example, a rapper asked if there were any Jews in the crowd. "Fuck Jews," he said. It's hard to imagine "Fuck Jews" as being anything other than a statement of anti-Semitism. And yet Norway's attorney general decided not to consider it hate speech on the grounds that it was possible the statement was "criticism of Israel."

"The Jews are our misfortune," the Nazi Party in Germany once proclaimed. Today, in a typical twist in which Israel has become the stand-in for the Jew, the German neo-Nazi party Die Rechte campaigns on the slogan "Israel is our misfortune." Perhaps the most shameless apologists will claim that this is "just" anti-Zionism, but it is clearly anti-Semitism in new clothes.

I am not saying that criticizing Israeli policy is anti-Semitic. Not in the least. Just as I believe that a crucial part of being an American patriot is not just defending America but insisting that it live up to its promise, part of being a Zionist means calling Israel to account when it falls short.

Many others can give you chapter and verse about the current policies of the Israeli government. As for me, I am deeply distressed about the stranglehold the rabbinate holds on Jewish life in Israel—a stranglehold I felt personally when young ultra-Orthodox men spit on me at the Western Wall in March 2019. I believe that the current government is betraying the six million murdered by cozying up to far-right nationalists, like Viktor Orbán, who has transformed Hungary into what he proudly calls an illiberal democracy while carrying out a state-sponsored campaign of Holocaust revisionism. I believe that Prime Minister Benjamin Netanyahu desecrated the Jewish state when he ushered the unapologetically racist party Otzma Yehudit into his governing coalition. Watching young Palestinians waiting at checkpoints makes me despair.

Pick up today's newspaper. There you can surely read about any number of Israel's policy disgraces. Better yet, listen in on a single hour of debate in the Knesset.

But to feel the need to explain or apologize excessively for this or that Israeli failing is to give in to the conundrum that Bob Dylan brilliantly exposed in "Neighborhood Bully," in which Israel is "criticized and condemned for being alive." Or as Susan Rice put it less poetically but just as clearly: "No country is immune to criticism, nor should it be. But when that criticism takes the form of singling out just one country, unfairly, bitterly and relentlessly, over and over and over, that's just wrong—and we all know it."

Anti-Zionism is not about criticizing Israeli policies or expressing concern about the direction Israel is heading. It is about the demonization and the delegitimization and, ultimately, the elimination of a single state that exists in the actual world.

Imagine a young couple talking about having children. They have legitimate questions to discuss with each other: Can we afford it? Is our apartment big enough? Do we want to change our life so radically? Do we want to become parents? Once they have the baby, though, that conversation becomes immoral.

To be an anti-Zionist in Poland before the Holocaust is one thing. To be one today is something else entirely. It is not to be ideologically opposed to an idea. It is to be against the largest Jewish community on the planet.

You can suggest that the current policies of the Jewish state betray Jewish values. You can claim that contemporary Zionism is not what our ancestors would have embraced. But you cannot erase the clear line of Jewish history that leads the Jewish people back to that land. It is as fundamental as our liberation from slavery, as core an idea as our covenant with God. That is part of the reason why 92 percent of American Jews identify themselves as "pro-Israel" even as a majority of them are critical of some Israeli government policies, according to a 2018 Mellman Group survey.

As Milton Steinberg wrote in "The Creed of an American Zionist": "The first error of the anti-Zionist is that he misconstrues Judaism." To the anti-Zionist, he writes, "Judaism is purely a religion, the Jews members of a church. Hence notions of a homeland and commonwealth are altogether inappropriate." In this, writes Steinberg, "he blunders again for lack of imagination. It escapes him that other Jews live in scenes different from his, and that circumstances alter cases. America is a uninational and, except for secondary cultures, a unicultural land. Judaism here naturally takes the form of a religio-cultural entity. But Poland, Rumania, and the Soviet Union are composed of many peoples, cultures, and nationalities. There Jews also constitute in law and public opinion a *nationality*."

That was written in *The Atlantic* in 1945. But it could just as easily have been written today. Only now, the anti-Zionists have decades more evidence—not just of the need for Israel but of the miracle of its ability to remain essentially liberal in an illiberal region. Yet they still oppose its existence.

Anti-Zionists will say that they are opposed to nationalism, yet they champion the Palestinian kind. They will say that they care about religious minorities, but they are curiously silent about the treatment of Uighurs in China or the forced modern exodus of Christians from the Middle East. They will say that they care about indigenous rights, yet they elide the inconvenient truth that there has been a Jewish presence in the historical land of Israel since the destruction of the Temple. They will say that Israel was established by foreign imperial powers, but they will ignore that modern India, say, was established in the same way. Somehow none of those who claim to oppose nationalism ever suggest dismantling India.

Anti-Zionists will say that they are fixated on Israel because they care about Palestinian refugees. But what do they say about the displacement of millions of Syrians? Or, for that matter, about the more than two million Palestinian refugees in Jordan, of whom more than 370,000 remain in refugee camps?

Often anti-Zionists will cite Israel's security and settlement policies as their justification for opposing the state itself. But if antidemocratic policies against Palestinians are what matters, they only matter insofar as Jews are involved. In Lebanon, there are around 450,000 Palestinians. More than 50 percent of them, according to the United Nations, live in the country's twelve refugee camps. In part that is because the state bars them by law from more than twenty professions, including from working as doctors, lawyers, engineers, or accountants.

Any honest person has to admit that there were and are injustices perpetrated by Israel. Israel, like all other nation-states, displaced people. In 1947, Israel accepted the United Nations Partition Plan and the Arabs did not.

Then, when Israel declared statehood in May 1948, the armies of five Arab states, cooperating with the grand mufti of Jerusalem, declared a war on Israel of genocidal intent, during which 750,000 Arabs fled or were expelled. The tragedy of this is undeniable.

That tragedy is compounded when you watch Israeli soldiers police, for example, the tiny Jewish outpost in Hebron. It is a source of enormous discomfort even if you know about the Arab pogrom in 1929 that ended many centuries of Jewish life in the town; even if you know that King David ruled there; even if you believe that the Cave of the Patriarchs is second only to the Temple Mount in its holiness. The suffering of the Palestinians there is a strain on the Jewish soul. Including mine.

But it would be obscene to claim that Israel's flaws are indistinguishable from the killing fields of Sudan or the depravity of the North Korean slave state. And yet it is the Jewish state that is singled out for condemnation again and again. According to UN Watch, between 2006 and 2016, the United Nations Human Rights Council condemned Israel on sixty-eight different occasions. The country with the next most was Syria, with twenty. North Korea had nine. China, Saudi Arabia, Pakistan: all zero.

Yet aside from a few tireless activists, columnists, and advocates, UN Watch's Hillel Neuer chief among them, this bias is rarely called out for what it is. "The finest trick of the devil," said Baudelaire, "is to persuade you that he does not exist." Likewise for anti-Zionism, whose adher-

ents have successfully persuaded the world that their ideology is not what it appears to be.

. . .

Anti-Zionism is not just anti-Semitism because of current reality. Anti-Zionism is also anti-Semitism because
of history.

In Jewish day school, we talked a lot about Hitler; at
lunch we played a dark game in which we'd wonder aloud
who would survive. At night I would have horrific dreams
about my family being hunted down. But I'm not sure I
ever heard my teachers mention Stalin's name, let alone
Lenin's. Considering that there were newly immigrated
Russian Jews in our school—kids who were picked on for
their accents and bad haircuts—the omission is puzzling.
We, the spoiled ones, had little idea what these families
had endured in the Soviet Union, what their parents had
sacrificed for a better life here.

So why did we know so much about Hitler and so little about the anti-Semitism that gripped the place now
called Russia? If it was a question of body count, Stalin's
was higher by far. Perhaps it was because many of our
grandparents had survived Hitler's death camps. Perhaps
it was because the American Jewish identification with
the political left made the oppression of Jews under the
Communists seem somehow less bad, or at least less
comfortable to discuss. The dream of a better world

speaks to Americans, and particularly Jewish Americans, in a way that blood-and-soil politics never will. Perhaps—as I would come to learn as an adult when I read about the Doctors' Plot or the Night of the Murdered Poets—it was because of the sordid and tragic role Jews play in this line of anti-Semitic history. Perhaps it was recoil from the overreach of McCarthyism.

Or maybe it was the happy result of massive American Jewish activism on behalf of Soviet Jews in the 1980s, which Gal Beckerman documents in his superb book *When They Come for Us, We'll Be Gone*. On December 6, 1987, at three years old, I, along with my parents and 250,000 others, marched in Washington, D.C., to demand freedom for Soviet Jewry. Ultimately, they were freed. The Iron Curtain fell. Perhaps because the good guys won, the devastation of Soviet anti-Semitism became a fast-fading memory.

But the nasty and long legacy of anti-Semitism on the political left is one very much worth remembering today. As many well-intentioned people look to understand why a very small but very vocal group of Jews seems as deeply opposed to Jewish interests as many of our community's enemies, these Jews ought to be understood in context, as part of a long history of left-wing anti-Semitic movements that successfully conscript Jews as agents in their own destruction.

The conversation inevitably begins with Marx. The debate about whether Marx was an anti-Semite largely focuses on his essay "On the Jewish Question," which contains lines like these: "What is the worldly religion of the Jew? Huckstering. What is his worldly God? Money." Some say these words can only be read as passionate anti-Semitism. Others say that Marx is merely ridiculing anti-Semitic tropes. Still others maintain that Marx means to point out that anti-Semitism itself rightly singles out traits to condemn—like capitalistic greed—but that he didn't mean that the Jews were somehow condemned. Some insist that it's all ironic.

I suggest reading the whole essay and judging for yourself. But the historical upshot of Marx's work is clear: The most important and enduring leftist philosopher succeeded in fundamentally identifying Jews with capitalism, the great evil of leftist ideologies. Much flows from that linkage. Namely, the focus of left-wing revolutionary movements on the particular evil of the Jews; the tendency for those movements to pretend otherwise; and the Jewish need inside those movements to prove that they are not, in fact, the source of all that is ill in a society.

Under Lenin's one-party state rule, this took the form of the Yevsektsiya, the Jewish section of the Bolshevik Party, run by—who else?—Jews. It was a perfect solution. The state could ban Judaism and criminalize Zionism, and Lenin could point to the fact of the Jewish section to prove that the Communists were actually philo-Semitic. Jews could join—and persecute other Jews—to prove that they were committed members of the party.

As Richard Pipes writes in *Russia Under the Bolshevik*

Regime, the Yevsektsiya "persecuted their own religion with exceptional zeal in order to prove the anti-Semites wrong." The war they waged was both a physical and a cultural one. Hebrew was outlawed; Jewish religious practice was forbidden. Rabbis were tormented or killed. And while every Jewish organization came under attack, the Zionist movement and its activists—those nefarious nationalists—were singled out for special violence.

The Jewish Communists who ran the Yevsektsiya, terrorizing their fellow Jews and demolishing Jewish politics and culture—what was in it for them? Surely some of these people truly believed that they were sacrificing some Jewish lives to save the greater number. Maybe some believed that at least they could protect themselves. Or perhaps they were craven. It must be the case that some were true believers in the Bolshevik vision.

Consider Esther Frumkin (born Chaya Malka Lifshits), one of the leaders of the Yevsektsiya, who also edited the Yiddish Communist newspaper *Der Emes* ("The Truth"). "If the Russian people begin to feel that we are partial to the Jews it will be harmful to Jews," she wrote. "The danger is that the masses may think that Judaism is exempt from anti-religious propaganda. Therefore, Jewish Communists must be even more ruthless with rabbis than non-Jewish Communists are with priests."

Of course in the end, as always, the regime those Jews served so zealously ultimately came for them, too. Esther Frumkin was arrested and imprisoned in 1938, along with other "unreconstructed Bundists" and "counterrevolutionary nationalists." She was sentenced to eight years in a detention camp; she died there in 1943. If you pick up a Marxist broadside today, you will see that she is hailed, still, as a hero.

The Yevsektsiya makes the Jews' bargain with the far left—a bargain that remains the same today—clear: The mutilating condition of being fully accepted is making war against anything that smacks of Jewish particularism, the boundaries of which are always unclear. Is it affinity for the State of Israel? Is it too much emphasis on Jewish themes in your plays? Or too many Jewish characters? Is it talking with your hands? The lines are always moving.

Stalin took things a step further than Lenin by combining a hatred of Jewish particularism with some degree of old-fashioned Russian anti-Semitism. Every aspect of Jewish culture, even Yiddish itself, which was the language of the Jewish Communists, had to be stripped of its Jewishness. Words were literally spelled differently to erase their Hebraic origins.

In 1941, Stalin officially conscripted his Jews into what was called the Jewish Ant-Fascist Committee. It was composed of many of the biggest celebrities—writers, actors, and poets—of the Soviet Union. The job of these Jews was twofold: acting as window dressing for the dear leader and eliciting support from American Jews in the fight against fascism.

Those Jews who worked tirelessly for Stalin? The tyrant ultimately determined that they were nothing more than agents of a "Zionist conspiracy." Three years after the end of the Holocaust, the committee chairman, Solomon Mikhoels, was murdered by Stalin's secret police. The death of Moscow's most famous Yiddish theater director awakened another member of the committee, the poet Peretz Markish, to Stalin's true nature: "Hitler wanted to destroy us physically; Stalin wants to do it spiritually." But in this, tragically, Markish was ultimately wrong. In what is now known as the Night of the Murdered Poets (Nathan Englander's excellent play about the events is called *The Twenty-Seventh Man*), nearly all of Stalin's Jewish loyalists, those members of the Jewish Anti-Fascist Committee, were executed by firing squad in Moscow's Lubyanka Prison on August 12, 1952. Peretz Markish was among them.

Year after year, as Israel proved its staying power, the Soviet propaganda war against Zionism and the Jews that had begun under Lenin and blossomed under Stalin was waged against an actual state and millions of Soviet Jews. That strategy only deepened after the Six-Day War of 1967, when Israel's shocking victory over the Soviet Union's Arab proxies, out of which grew its long-standing alliance with the United States, gave the Soviet Union more reason than ever to demonize the Jewish state and the Soviet Jews it accused of having dual loyalty. In waging war against Israel, through its proxies and its propaganda, the Soviet Union could boost those Soviet-aligned Arab nations humiliated by their defeat, undermine American interests in the Middle East, and justify its persecution of Soviet Jews. Theirs was a three-pronged formulation for opposing Israel, America, and diaspora Jews that continues to guide the thinking of many leftists today.

As the Soviet-born Jewish scholar Izabella Tabarovsky has shown in a series of insightful essays, the Soviet Union was tireless and brutal in its efforts. It produced hundreds of books and thousands of articles attacking Zionism, many of which compared it directly with Nazism. This propaganda was translated into dozens of languages and reached new audiences thanks to foreign radio broadcasts as well. The KGB called it Operation SIG (for *Sionistskiye Gosudarstva,* or "Zionist Governments"). "In developing their ideas, Soviet ideologues relied for inspiration on *The Protocols of the Elders of Zion,* on the ideas of classic religious anti-Semitism, and even *Mein Kampf,* but adopted them to the Marxist framework by substituting the idea of a global anti-Soviet Zionist conspiracy for a specifically Jewish one," Tabarovsky writes. "Jewish power became Zionist power. The rich and conniving Jewish bankers controlling money, politicians, and the media became the rich and conniving Zionists. The Jew as the anti-Christ became the Jew as the anti-Soviet. Instead of the Jew as the devil, they presented the Zionist as a Nazi."

There was more than one willing audience for this message. In countries where anti-Semitism was deeply rooted, like Russia and Romania, the message was a reverberation of very old themes. The KGB found new audiences in Muslim countries bitter over their loss to Israel, and in African nations that quite understandably hated racism and colonialism, which is what relentless Soviet propaganda campaigns insisted Zionism was.

Protocols was translated into Arabic and distributed throughout the Muslim world. Meantime, a willing partner was found in the person of Yasser Arafat. (The sordid details of the relationship between the Soviets and Arafat can be found in *Red Horizons,* the memoir of Ion Mihai Pacepa, the highest-ranking intelligence officer ever to have defected from the Eastern Bloc.) Unable to beat Israel in a conventional battle, the Jewish nation's enemies looked to terrorism and information warfare as new fronts, and the Soviets brilliantly and successfully turned the United Nations into a forum for their proxy war. In 1974, Arafat gave a speech at the U.N. perfectly articulating the fruits of Operation SIG. "The old world order is crumbling before our eyes, as imperialism, colonialism, neo-colonialism, and racism, the chief form of which is Zionism, ineluctably perish," he promised.

"Zionism is an ideology that is imperialist, colonialist, racist; it is profoundly reactionary and discriminatory; it is united with anti-Semitism in its retrograde tenets and is, when all is said and done, another side of the same base coin," Arafat proclaimed. Three decades later, my university professors said the same thing.

And Arafat, in what has become an idée fixe of the modern left, drew a stark distinction between Judaism and Zionism. "While we maintain our opposition to the colonialist Zionist movement," he said, "we respect the Jewish faith. Today, almost one century after the rise of the Zionist movement, we wish to warn of its increasing danger to the Jews of the world, to our Arab people, and to world peace and security. For Zionism encourages the Jew to emigrate out of his homeland and grants him an artificially created nationality."

Others followed Arafat's lead. The next year, the dictator Idi Amin called for the United States to "rid their society of the Zionists" and for "the extinction of Israel as a state." Then, in 1975, this Cold War proxy battle peaked with the success of the "Zionism is racism" resolution in the United Nations. "There were ghosts haunting the Third Committee that day: The ghosts of Hitler and Goebbels and Julius Streicher, grinning with delight to hear, not only Israel, but Jews as such denounced in language which would have provoked hysterical applause at any Nuremberg rally," wrote the British journalist and academic Goronwy Rees, who had witnessed the debate over the resolution. "For the fundamental thesis advocated by the supporters of the resolution . . . was that to be a Jew, and to be proud of it, and to be determined to preserve the right to be a Jew, is to be an enemy of the human race."

The notorious resolution, which declared that "Zionism is a form of racism and racial discrimination," was ultimately repealed in 1991, but the damage was done, as evidenced by my interaction with a perfectly naïve undergraduate on the New York City subway a little more than a decade later.

"The abomination of anti-Semitism has been given the appearance of international sanction," Daniel Patrick Moynihan, then the American ambassador to the United Nations, said on the day the resolution was passed. "The terrible lie that has been told here today will have terrible consequences." I'm not sure he could have imagined how normative the lie has become.

Could he have imagined that in 2019 the international edition of *The New York Times* would mistakenly run a cartoon of Israeli prime minister Benjamin Netanyahu as a dog with a Magen David collar leading a blind Donald Trump wearing a kippah? A cartoon that could have been cooked up in 1970 by the KGB? Would he have been able to imagine young anti-Zionist Jewish lesbians declaring, as they did in June 2019 in Washington, D.C., that "when other Jews conflate anti-Semitism with anti-Zionism and anti-nationalism, it makes us angry and sad. It makes us feel like we are further from true liberation. To be a Jew is to have a history of trauma and oppression." As if *that* is what it means to be a Jew. Could he have imagined that in the most elite spaces across the country, people declare, unthinkingly, that Israel is a racist state and that Zionism is racism, without realizing that they are participating in a Soviet conspiracy, without realizing that they are aligning themselves with the greatest mass murderers in modern history?

If Hitler is responsible for the big lie told about the Jews in the twentieth century, the Soviet Union is responsible for generating the big lie being told about the Jews in the twenty-first. And as the Israeli writer Yossi Klein Halevi has said, the "existential threat" of the anti-Zionist lie "is that it declares war on the story of the Jewish people."

. . .

At the same time that progressives have, knowingly or unknowingly, embraced the Soviet lie that Israel is a colonialist outpost that should be opposed, the idea of intersectionality has taken powerful hold over the progressive left. So important has intersectionality become that presidential candidates like Kirsten Gillibrand have declared that the future is not just female, it is intersectional, as she recently put it on Twitter. Unfortunately, this is an idea that has been weaponized at the expense of Jews and has hampered our ability to fight anti-Semitism alongside those who should be our allies.

That was never the intent of intersectionality. The idea behind this theory of oppression is deeply appealing because it observes something that is obviously true. The legal scholar Kimberlé Crenshaw named it in 1989 to explain how people with multiple minority identities can be discriminated against in multiple ways. Specifically: When black women at General Motors were denied jobs, was it because they were black or because they were women? Or both? That was the challenge in the key case Crenshaw cites, *DeGraffenreid v. General Motors* (1976), in which five women sued GM for hiring discrimination. At the time they sued, GM had jobs for black men on the factory floor and for white women as secretaries. But neither job could be filled by these black women. For one job, they were too female. For the other, they were too black.

At that time, American law put issues of race and gender into separate buckets, so the case was dismissed and the women were denied justice. As Crenshaw has written: "Why? Because the court believed that black women should not be permitted to combine their race and gender claims into one. Because they could not prove that what happened to them was just like what happened to white women or black men, the discrimination that happened to these black women fell through the cracks."

If intersectionality simply functioned as a framework for understanding the world—why certain people (white men) can be doubly blessed while others (black women) can be doubly compromised—I'd be the first to suggest it. But in reality, intersectionality tends to function as a caste system, the reverse of the caste system that has dominated Western history until five minutes ago. If white, straight men have historically sat at the top of the hierarchy, now those with the most oppressions (black, transgender, disabled) are located at the top, and, furthermore, are granted a greater claim to truth and morality than those with more racial or gender or sexual or physical advantage. In this ladder, which leaves no room for appreciating how the powerful have long scapegoated and used the Jews, Jews are right at the bottom, just one rung above white, heterosexual males. Many Jews, after all, can present as white. Ergo: They cannot be victims.

Intersectionality is why any time the neo-Nazis attack Jews, progressives are reliably outspoken, but when the perpetrator is an Islamist or a black Farrakhan supporter, many of those same people avert their gaze. Intersectionality is why feminist groups have so much to say about Israel's actions (as a white colonialist state) and yet nothing to say when gays are hunted down by Hamas or hanged from construction cranes in Iran. The same logic applies to the deafening silence about the burka, say, or female genital mutilation. If you can tangentially blame the West, the West will be blamed. The racism of this is as transparent as it is ugly.

I know of a student at a leading liberal arts college who recently took a class about the Holocaust. The discussion turned to writer and Holocaust survivor Elie Wiesel. A classmate called Wiesel "privileged." Why? Because he "was a white, able-bodied man." This is your brain on intersectionality.

Anyone who buys into this caste system inevitably diminishes the threat against Jews, as if it's a zero-sum competition for who has suffered the most. It is how, in the wake of the Poway shooting, a leftist Jewish writer tweeted the following: "antiSemitic murder of Jews pales in comparison to systematic racial violence against Blacks and others." It's an astonishing reaction.

According to the FBI, Jews have been the victims of a majority of religiously motivated hate crimes in the United States every single year since 1995. Attacks on Jews continue to dwarf anti-Muslim hate crimes even in an era when the Trump administration has explicitly pursued anti-Muslim policies. Yet outside of high-profile spectacles of far-right violence, there seems to be barely any awareness—or perhaps it is willful blindness—of the degree to which Jews are targeted by Americans of all races and creeds because of who they are.

Because Jews have been successfully whitewashed, put solely into the class of the privileged, they are not allowed to criticize anyone from historically victimized groups—even when people from those groups happen to be the ones doing the victimizing. Criticize Steve King's anti-Semitism and racism all you want. But criticize Women's March leader Linda Sarsour for her repeated anti-Semitic outbursts? Criticize her and you are not just rendered racist and a misogynist and an Islamophobe in league with Trump, you stand accused of putting her life at risk for trying to hold her accountable for promoting anti-Semitism.

In a righteous attempt to right historic wrongs, intersectionality replicates the same logic (some groups are inherently better; some are inherently worse) that made intersectionality relevant in the first place. It retribalizes us, preventing us from treating people as individuals—an idea as un-American as the right-wing notion that white Americans are somehow more truly American than those who aren't.

. . .

So this is where we are. Jews who refuse to undergo progressive conversion are going to be smeared, increasingly often, as handmaidens of white supremacy, at home and abroad. In the meantime, the far right will continue to insist that Jews are betrayers of the white majority by, among other things, voting Democratic and supporting immigration. Given the primacy of race in the American story, perhaps we should not be surprised to see that the Jews' role hinges on the question of "whiteness." That is: The left says we are white; the right says we trick people into thinking we are.

The left transforms Jews into enforcers and beneficiaries of white supremacy in three fundamental ways:

First, American Jews are white because many of us are of Eastern Europe heritage and have the appearance that comes with it. We present as white in situations with police, employers, and mortgage providers. Also, we have largely made it in America. That success has rendered us incapable of being victims.

Second, American Jews are turned into white racists because we support Israel, a state about which an enormous lie has been told. Namely, that it is a white colonialist enterprise and an expression of American imperialism. Never mind that more than half of the Jews who live in that state are refugees from the Middle East; that the country's founders fled racial and religious oppression in imperial Russia; that it was the only Western nation to bring oppressed people out of Africa en masse to liberation; and that it gave a chance at new life to hundreds of thousands of Holocaust survivors when few other nations were willing to take them in.

Third, we are white racists because we criticize anti-Semites, including when those anti-Semites happen to be people of color. And by speaking out against anti-Semitism without making exception for those in oppressed groups, the Jews are rendered the oppressors.

Interestingly, the people who are most emphatic about turning Jews white are, in fact, other white liberals. As Zach Goldberg, a political science graduate student at Georgia State University, has shown, white liberals' sympathy for Jews and Israel has become far more conditional in recent years. "Having made a full recovery from the Holocaust, Jews are no longer the downtrodden collective that white liberals can readily sympathize with. Other groups lower on the privilege hierarchy and less tainted by association with whiteness now have priority," he writes. "To see how this logic extends to Israel consider that the same empathic outrage over the bigoted persecution by the 'privileged' against the vulnerable that informs the changing policy positions on domestic issues is extended out to the international arena where Israel is a fixture of every moral drama," Goldberg continues. "As Jews have become beacons of whiteness in the liberal political imagination—to the point that Israel is considered a white state despite having a slight nonwhite majority—they have come to be associated with an oppressor class."

This is why anyone who dared criticize the leaders of the Women's March, Tamika Mallory and Linda Sarsour, was chided as racist-adjacent at best, while these women appeared in glossy women's magazines as modern-day Rosie the Riveters, with no mention of their embrace of the anti-Semite, misogynist, and homophobe Louis Farrakhan.

The Jews as white supremacists is the modern formulation of the old rule. Jews are transformed into whatever a given society hates most. Right now, on the progressive left, that thing is whiteness. Not, mind you, that many Jews can't pass as white: Many can and do. But that is not what is at stake. The issue is the forcible conversion of Jews into oppressors.

I have come to think of this as the left-wing version of replacement theory. If the replacement theory of the far right posits that Jews are the tools of immigrants and brown and black people aiming to supplant the white majority, replacement theory on the left posits that Jews are handmaidens of white supremacy and its active embodiment in Israel. This replacement theory is constructed based on the lie that Jews have no indigenous claim to the land of Israel—a claim easily refuted by archaeology, history, and ancestry.

Yet this lie has become pervasive. A recent *New York Times* story about Jesus claimed that the founder of Christianity "was most likely a Palestinian man with dark skin." This is absurd and ahistorical. First, Jesus was a Jew. Second, the region where he lived was known at the time as Judea. The paper corrected the widely disseminated error, but perhaps did not fully understand why the mistake had been made in the first place. It was made because "Palestinian" has become a synonym for indigeneity in the Holy Land.

Of course, two peoples—Jews and Palestinians—can both have an indigenous claim. I think they can and believe that they do. But in the left-wing version of replacement theory, the Jews are the ones who have replaced the Palestinians. This is why a Palestinian identity must be photoshopped onto an ancient Jew (to call Jesus a Jew is to betray his "older" and "original" identity as a Palestinian). And it is why, in this view of the world, Zionism is not the return of a native people but a colonial replacement.

This is the replacement theory behind Marc Lamont Hill's breathtaking comments that "Mizrahi Jew" is a fake identity, constructed by Zionists "as a means of detaching them from Palestinian identity." The Temple University professor should tell that to the Jews of Afghanistan and Iraq, who lived for centuries in those countries as second-class citizens.

Left-wing replacement theory lurks behind comments like these, from Michigan's Democratic congresswoman Rashida Tlaib: "There's always kind of a calming feeling, I tell folks, when I think of the Holocaust, and the tragedy of the Holocaust, and the fact that it was my ancestors—Palestinians—who lost their land and some lost their lives, their livelihood, their human dignity, their existence in many ways, have been wiped out, and some people's passports. And just all of it was in the name of trying to create a safe haven for Jews, post–the Holocaust, post–the tragedy and the horrific persecution of Jews across the world at that time. And I love the fact that it was my ancestors that provided that, right, in many ways. But they did it in a way that took their human dignity away and it was forced on them."

In presenting the Jewish presence in the land of Israel as mere compensation for the Holocaust and insisting that the Arabs welcomed Jewish survivors of Hitler's genocide, Tlaib repeats two enormous lies whose singular purpose is to underscore that only Arabs, and not Jews, are native to the land both groups cherish. If Jews are usurpers with no legitimate claim, then Jews are necessarily "replacing" the natural, Palestinian order of things. Perhaps that is why Tlaib supports a single (Palestinian) state rather than a two-state solution.

The Republicans weaponized Tlaib's comments; anything less would have been political malpractice. But focusing on the GOP's reaction, as House Speaker Nancy Pelosi did, is to ignore what the congresswoman actually said. If somebody told you that they got a "calming feeling" about the fact that their ancestors "lost their land and some lost their lives, their livelihood, their human dignity, their existence in many ways, have been wiped out," either that person is a saint or that person is a liar.

The question is why so many people are invested in covering up such a lie.

CHAPTER 5

RADICAL ISLAM

In 1298, Jews in Europe were burned at the stake over a wafer. The violence—the worst against European Jews since the Crusades—began on April 20 in Röttingen, when the town's Jews were accused of stealing Eucharist wafers for the purpose of defiling them. According to one source, the Jews tortured a wafer until it bled. This libelous fiction set off a series of pogroms that swept nearly 150 towns across Austria and Germany. Over the course of a few years, some one hundred thousand Jews were murdered.

Look back at the history of church doctrine and this drawn-out massacre begins to make much more sense. In 1215 the church officially defined the concept of transubstantiation: The wafer and the wine were no longer symbolic but the actual body and blood of Christ. What followed were tales of Jews torturing these wafers, crucifying them, making them literally bleed.

I open this chapter with this particularly absurdist and brutal Christian bloodletting, known to us now as the *Rintfleisch* massacres, to make it absolutely clear that though today it is radical Islam that is exceptional in its animosity toward the Jewish people, until the twentieth century it was Christianity that was responsible for the murder of more Jews than any other ideology on the planet. If I were writing this book in the Middle Ages, this chapter would surely focus on the particularly lethal threat that that iteration of the religion posed to world Jewry.

Religions, like politics and cultures, are plastic, not made of stone. They can and do transform. Protestants and Catholics slaughtered one another in the Thirty Years' War, in part over whether that wafer was flesh or a carbohydrate. The question raised by that war, in which eight million lost their lives: How can people with fundamentally different religious worldviews live together without killing one another? The American experiment has provided one almost miraculously successful answer. Where once Catholics and Protestants fought to the death, now they get brunch.

That religions are not static, that different doctrines and texts and heroic figures and interpretations get emphasized and de-emphasized over time (there are terrible lines about Jews in both the Koran and the New Testament), should give us hope.

And yet various constituencies with obvious political agendas pretend that these sensitive, gray matters are entirely black and white. Some on the political right seek to cleanse Christianity of its bloody history toward Jews and argue that Islam is an exceptionally violent creed. And some on the political left go to great pains to portray anti-Semitism as a uniquely Christian phenomenon, eager to paint contemporary Islam as fundamentally misunderstood. The first is a denial of history; it purifies Europe's ugly past as a way to justify ugly anti-Muslim bigotries and cruel policies in the present. The second is a denial of our difficult present reality; it paves the way for an uglier future.

Neither version is true. The truth, as often, lies somewhere in between. As many scholars of Islam, most notably Bernard Lewis (*The Jews of Islam*), have convincingly shown, for most of history, it was Muslim lands, not Christian ones, that were more hospitable to Jews. As Lewis succinctly put it: The Jewish experience under Islam was "never as bad as in Christendom at its worst, nor ever as good as in Christendom at its best."

Under Islam, Jews lived as *dhimmis*—a "tolerated" second-class minority. They had to pay a high tax for protection. They could not build synagogues or drink wine in public or ride horses or offer evidence in court. It was not the Nazis who invented the idea of marking the Jew: The Jews had to designate themselves publicly beginning in the eighth century. According to the United States Holocaust Museum, "Under Caliph Haroun al-Rashid (807 C.E.), Jews in Baghdad had to wear yellow belts or fringes. Under Caliph al-Mutawakkil (847–61),

Jews wore a patch in the shape of a donkey, while Christians wore a figure in the shape of swine. In 1005, Jews in Egypt were ordered to wear bells on their clothes."

Suffice it to say, this was no golden age. But neither was it a dark one. As Robert Wistrich, the late scholar of anti-Semitism, wrote in his 2002 report *Muslim Anti-Semitism: A Clear and Present Danger:* "Despite the servitude and discrimination implicit in the *dhimmi* status of the premodern era, Jews under Islam were nonetheless in a relatively better position than their coreligionists in Christian lands. They did not, for instance, carry the theological odium of Christ killers as a mark of Cain on their brows. The more self-confident medieval Muslims did not feel the same compulsion as their Christian counterparts to negate Judaism as a religion, to engage in endless denigratory polemics against its validity, or to replace the 'Old Covenant' with a 'new' Israel of the spirit. . . . The discrimination they did suffer under Islam was qualitatively far more benign than their exclusion and demonization in medieval Christianity."

In other words, there was systemic prejudice against Jewish people, but there was not anti-Semitism in the sense of a conspiracy theory in which Jews spread evil in the world. And yet today, nowhere is that conspiracy more widely believed, and more publicly proclaimed, than in the Muslim world. What happened? How did a region in which Jews lived for generations become almost entirely *Judenrein*?

Like most of the developments that made our modern

world, the shift happened in the nineteenth century. Scholars point to a combination of factors: the rise of nationalism, including political Zionism; the threat that Western liberalism and globalization posed to traditional Islam; and colonialism.

European colonialism brought large numbers of Christians to the region as the Islamic colonialism presided over by the Ottoman Empire was waning. These foreign diplomats, religious figures, and bureaucrats did not leave their dangerous ideas about Jews, including that of the blood libel, behind. One of the first blood libels in the Muslim world occurred in 1840 Damascus, more than 350 years after Italian Jews were blamed for the disappearance of young Simon of Trent. In this case, the Jews stood accused of killing a Christian friar, an Italian known as Father Thomas. Nine of the city's most famous Jews were arrested and tortured; their teeth and hair pulled out, their skin burned. *The Times* of London editorialized about the events thusly: It is "one of the most important cases ever submitted to the notice of the civilized world." If the Jews were guilty of the crime, "then the Jewish religion must at once disappear from the face of the earth." This, from a newspaper published after the Enlightenment in the center of civilized Europe.

But it would be inaccurate to say that these anti-Semitic ideas were a pure transplant from the West. They could not have taken root in the East had there not been fertile soil. That soil was found not just in the literal text of the Koran, in which particular verses were now far more salient, but in the religious teachings of figures like the thirteenth-century scholar Ibn Taymiyyah, which had newfound, dangerous relevance.

As early as 1933, the grand mufti of Jerusalem made his support for the Nazis clear via German officials in Jerusalem. Amin al-Husseini's 1941 meeting with Hitler is well known; less known is the fact that the mufti recruited actual soldiers for the Nazi Party's Handschar division. As the mufti strengthened his ties to Hitler's regime, the Nazis pumped their propaganda into the region. Jeffrey Herf's *Nazi Propaganda for the Arab World* shows how Nazism combined with a particular interpretation of Islam to produce a particularly toxic brew: "It was a selective reading of the Koran and a focus on the anti-Jewish currents within Islam, combined with Nazi denunciations of Western imperialism and Soviet Communism, that offered Nazi propaganda its points of entry to Arabs in North Africa, Egypt, Palestine, Syria, Lebanon, and Iraq and to Muslims in the Middle East in general."

In 1948, the establishment of the State of Israel—and the failure of multiple Arab armies to defeat the fledgling nation—only supercharged the hostility. Then, two years later, Sayyid Qutb, the father of Islamic fundamentalism and Osama bin Laden's intellectual godfather, published "Our Struggle with the Jews," a document whose genocidal logic continues to grip minds not just in the Middle East but all over the globe.

Qutb's argument goes like this: The Jews are not just

the agents of all modern evils—Western civilization, nationalism, communism, feminism, and so on. They have also been the enemies of Islam since as far back as the seventh century. To return Islamic civilization to its true roots—the only real way to defeat the West—the Jews, the chief symbol of the West and of modernity, have to be wiped out. Qutb despised America in particular, having spent six months as a graduate student in Colorado in 1949. Consider his view of jazz, though his riff on American women is nearly as hateful: "This is that music that Negroes invented to satisfy their primitive inclinations, as well as their desire to be noisy on the one hand and to excite bestial tendencies on the other."

You can imagine how Qutb's message about the Jews and the West resonated following Israel's shocking victory in 1967, at which point the Soviet Union began pumping its own malicious propaganda into the region, along with the arms it poured into Egypt to fight its proxy war against capitalism and the United States by targeting Israel.

Today the Muslim world is almost entirely Jew-free. The biggest Jewish community in the Middle East outside Israel is in Iran, which boasts around 8,500 people—less than the Jewish population of Alabama. In Egypt, there are fewer than twenty Jews. In Iraq, where once a third of Baghdad's population was Jewish, five remain. A man named Zablon Simintov is the only remaining Jew in all of Afghanistan.

Some 850,000 Jews, many from Middle Eastern communities that predated Islam by hundreds of years, were expelled in the wake of the establishment of the State of Israel. Soon, the region that gave birth to Christianity could be almost Christian-free as well, the result of an ongoing modern-day exodus from Islamist violence. And yet, despite the lack of almost any Jews and, increasingly, of other religious minorities, the anti-Semitism gushing out of this part of the world is more vicious than ever.

Fouad Ajami, the late Middle East scholar, called the ideologies roiling the Middle East a "malignant trilogy" of "anti-Americanism, anti-Semitism and anti-modernism." I see that trilogy as a result of another: Nazism, Soviet communism, and a radical interpretation of Islam. When you appreciate this alchemy, you can understand how the original Hamas charter from 1988, only recently revised, claimed that the Jews orchestrated the French and Russian Revolutions and both world wars.

Bernard Lewis, Ajami's teacher, wrote this of the region's anti-Semitism: "The volume of anti-Semitic books and articles published, the size and number of editions and impressions, the eminence and authority of those who write, publish and sponsor them, their place in school and college curricula, their role in the mass media, would all seem to suggest that classical anti-Semitism is an essential part of Arab intellectual life at the present time—almost as much as happened in Nazi Germany, and considerably more than in late nineteenth and early twentieth century France." He wrote those words in 1986. Perhaps the scholar could have imagined how bad things would get, but I suspect even he could not have foreseen how anti-Semitism has truly spread "like a cancer" throughout the Muslim world, as Fareed Zakaria recently put it in *The Washington Post.*

No one does a better job of exposing how normative Jew hating is in the Middle East than the Middle East Media Research Institute (MEMRI), which translates foreign-language media reports into English. It is a bone-chilling experience to look at MEMRI's website and Twitter feed, but it is an essential one. (Neil Kressel's book *"The Sons of Pigs and Apes"* gathers some of the worst examples.)

The hate comes from state leaders and is not limited to Arabic-speaking nations. Look no further than Iran, whose supreme leader, Ayatollah Ali Khamenei, regularly says things like this: "This barbaric, wolflike, and infanticidal regime of Israel which spares no crime has no cure but to be annihilated." It comes from popular Islamist movements: A regular Muslim Brotherhood talking point these days stems from the *hadith* that proclaims that Judgment Day "will not come until the Muslims fight the Jews and kill them." It comes even from politicians in Muslim countries that until recently were considered liberal. Nabih Berri, the Speaker of the Parliament in Lebanon, was recently quoted in a Lebanese article titled "How to Recognize a Jew." Berri gave the following advice: "If you see a pregnant woman, get close to her and toss a piece of gold near her or at her feet. If the fetus jumps out from his mother's womb and grabs the gold, you know he is a Jew."

Perhaps most potently, it comes from the press—on television and radio, in newspapers, and, of course, through social media. In Egypt in 2002, for example, a forty-one-episode series that ran during the whole month of Ramadan was called *Horseman Without a Horse*. The theme of the series was the Zionist conspiracy to control the world; the producers openly acknowledged that they had been inspired by *The Protocols of the Elders of Zion*. The star of the show and its co-writer, Mohamed Sobhi, said that Zionism "has controlled the world since the dawn of history." *The New York Times* estimated that tens of millions of people tuned in.

This is not an unusual view of the power of the Jewish people. The feminist Ayaan Hirsi Ali wrote of her own experience growing up in Saudi Arabia in her memoir, *Infidel*. Ali, born Muslim, had never met a Jew, but she knew from a young age that they were the root of all evil. "In Saudi Arabia, everything bad was the fault of the Jews," she recalled. "When the air conditioner broke or suddenly the tap stopped running, the Saudi women next door used to say the Jews did it. The children next door were taught to pray for the health of their parents and the destruction of the Jews. Later, when we went to school, our teachers lamented at length all the evil things Jews had done and planned to do against Muslims. When they were gossiping, the women next door used to say,

'She's ugly, she's disobedient, she's a whore—she's sleeping with a Jew.'" As I write these words, an Egyptian actor and writer named Hesham Mansour, who has more than 800,000 followers on Twitter, is going on a tear: "jews controlled the space time continuum" and "Refer the Da Vinci code movie, the satanic rape scene underground, under the star of David, to know what jews do to women. All women." At last he reaches the natural conclusion: "Now lets kill some jews."

Given that anti-Semitism is a normative message in a large part of the world, it should not come as any surprise that a 2014 ADL survey, which looked at attitudes toward Jews in one hundred countries around the world, found that only 54 percent of the global population has heard of the Holocaust. That's a staggering enough fact on its own. Until you read that only 8 percent of respondents in the Middle East and North Africa had heard of the Holocaust and believed it had actually happened.

A 2008 Pew poll of twenty-four countries found that only seven of those nations had majorities or pluralities with a positive rating of Jews. America, for example, had 77 percent favorable. In Lebanon, by contrast, 97 percent of people were reported to have a negative view of Jews. In Egypt, 95 percent of people viewed Jews unfavorably. In Jordan, 96 percent did. And in Turkey and Pakistan, 76 percent.

In most parts of the world, more education is correlated with less anti-Semitism. But perhaps the most disheartening statistic of all is that, according to the most recent ADL Global 100 survey, that rule of thumb does not apply to the Middle East and North Africa. There, the more educated respondents were *more* likely to be anti-Semitic.

I could go on, but what is most relevant to this project is not documenting every depressing statistic, but understanding how these ideas travel across borders in an era in which literal borders are ever more porous and online borders are largely nonexistent. Just as classical anti-Semitism once traveled from the West to the East, today a brew of anti-Semitism, anti-liberalism, anti-Americanism, and anti-Zionism is moving in the opposite direction. And too many of the people who should be fighting against this contagion are either hastening its spread or looking the other way.

. . .

Between 2010 and 2016, an estimated 3.7 million Muslims migrated to Europe, according to the Pew Research Center. In Germany, after an influx of 850,000 Muslim migrants, the number of Muslims living in the country increased by roughly 2 percent to nearly 5 million, or 6 percent of the population. In the same period, 530,000 Muslims migrated to France; now 5.7 million Muslims constitute 8.8 percent of the French population. The number of Muslims living in the United Kingdom increased during those six years by roughly 20 percent to

4.1 million (6.3 percent of the population). Overall, Muslims make up roughly 5 percent of the population of Europe (some 26 million people). By 2050, according to some estimates, that number could double. By contrast, there are 1.4 million Jews in all of Europe.

When I think about these new entrants into Europe, I think about Alan Kurdi. For a few days, it seemed everyone knew his name. He was the three-year-old Syrian Kurdish boy in the red T-shirt who drowned in the Mediterranean Sea. The photograph of his tiny, lifeless body washed up on the beach of Bodrum, Turkey, woke up the world for a brief moment in September 2015, until most people went back to checking Facebook. The Kurdi family of four had boarded an inflatable boat along with eight other people in an attempt to reach Kos, a Greek island, and make their way, they hoped, to Canada.

Not all of those coming into Europe are literally fleeing for their lives. But given the countries they are coming from—Syria, Afghanistan, Somalia—it is a good bet that they are about as unlucky in the circumstances of their birth as I am lucky. I am also part of a religious tradition in which welcoming the stranger is bound up with our idea of God. The phrase that is repeated again and again in the Bible insists that we should not oppress a stranger, because we were strangers in the land of Egypt. The origin story of Judaism's founding father, Abraham, tells us that when he welcomes strangers at his tent—that most Middle Eastern of traditions—those strangers turn out to be angels. I also am intensely aware that I enjoy the freedoms I do because my own family once left a hostile Europe for a better life in America.

For both of these reasons, I have a deep, visceral reaction in favor of welcoming newcomers. I also have faith in the idea that their families, like mine and so many other immigrants', can discover a kind of compromise position that healthy liberal democracies allow: adapting to the cultural mores of their new countries while preserving their own communities and the best of their traditions.

Were Germany to turn away asylum seekers, it would "not be my country," Angela Merkel said in 2015 to justify her decision to open and keep open Germany's doors—a statement, given the country's history, that moved and resonated with me. I hope she was right when she promised, again and again, *Wir schaffen das,* "We can manage." And yet looking at the impact that these newcomers have had on European countries and their Jews—and what the European experience might portend for America—there is reason to worry.

· · ·

Let's assume that ideas matter and that we should trust people when they tell us what they think and believe about the world.

Just as it would have been ridiculous to assume that nineteenth-century European colonialists would have left behind their affinity for the blood libel when they went east, it is just as ridiculous to imagine that these newcomers would check their ideas at the border of the West.

Muslims across Europe are far more anti-Semitic than the general European population. A 2015 survey by the Anti-Defamation League broke down the numbers country by country. In Germany, 56 percent of Muslims hold anti-Semitic views, compared with 16 percent of the total population. In France, it is 49 percent to 17 percent. In the U.K., it is 54 percent to 12 percent.

So it should not be surprising to hear, for example, about Imam Said Abu Hafs's March 2019 sermon at the Islamic Center of Kaiserslautern, Germany, called "The Position of the Jews Towards Islam," in which he said of the Jews, "One of their wicked ways to fight Islam was to tear apart the unity of Muslims" and "It is well-known and does not need any further explanation that they are the most renowned of all people for their miserliness and love of money" and "They are enamored with gold. They have been arrogant, especially their rabbis and their leaders. They would enslave people."

And yet it is very hard to absorb the extent of Islamist anti-Semitism in Europe. Partly it is because Muslims in Europe are *themselves* subjected to systemic bigotry and discrimination, not to mention economic and social challenges. Partly it is because telling the truth about the depth of the problem opens one up to accusations of Islamophobia and xenophobia. That is why this deeply uncomfortable problem is severely underreported. And yet the existing reporting and data buttresses an inescapable theme: It is dangerous to be a Jew in Europe.

Start with France. Muslims outnumber Jews in that country ten to one, but in 2017 almost 40 percent of hate crimes motivated by race or religion targeted Jews. (In 2018, anti-Semitic attacks increased by 74 percent, with nearly 550 incidents. And those are only the ones that were reported.) Jews are twenty-five times more likely to be attacked than Muslims in France. "Anti-Semitism is spreading like a poison, like a venom," Christophe Castaner, France's interior minister, said this February.

In the Netherlands, the country's top watchdog group monitoring anti-Semitism, CIDI, estimates that in a given year, Muslims and Arabs are the perpetrators of 70 percent of anti-Semitic attacks. In 2018, the group reported a record 19 percent increase in anti-Semitic incidents.

It is not just anti-Semitism that has been imported by these new Europeans. More than 52 percent of British Muslims think that homosexuality should be illegal, according to a 2018 report from Ipsos MORI. In Birmingham, a city in which more than one resident in five is Muslim, some primary schools have stopped teaching courses promoting LGBT tolerance because of passionate protests from parents. Among British Muslims, more believe that Jews carried out 9/11 than trust that it was the work of Al Qaeda, according to a survey carried out by the Policy Exchange think tank.

In May of 2019, Germany's Federal Office for the Protection of the Constitution, or BfV, released a report
called "Anti-Semitism in Islamism." It documented a
slew of incidents, the sorts of things that have now become part of regular life in the country. In April 2016, a
woman in Berlin was wearing a necklace with an Israel-
shaped pendant. Two men of Arab descent said to her,
"You fucking Jews! You are the scum of the earth." In
December 2017, a Jewish high schooler was attacked by
an Arab classmate who said, "You are child murderers,
you should have your heads cut off." Or in perhaps the
most memorable case, a young Israeli Arab man decided
to wear a kippah in public as an "experiment," since he
was skeptical of the idea that there was indeed anti-
Semitism in Berlin. He was set upon by three men in the
hip neighborhood of Prenzlauer Berg. *"Yahudi,"* they
shouted, the word for "Jew" in Arabic. One whipped him
with a belt.

In Sweden, the country's eighteen thousand Jews have
gotten used to the attacks. In the southern city of Malmö,
in which at least 20 percent of the population is Muslim
and there remain some one thousand Jews, things have
gotten particularly bad. Shneur Kesselman is the only
Hasidic rabbi in the city, and thus is easily identifiable.
He has been the victim of more than a hundred verbal
and physical assaults. That astonishing number begins to
make more sense when you read about the political climate in Malmö. In December 2017, for example, after
Donald Trump announced that the United States would

recognize Jerusalem as Israel's capital, hundreds of demonstrators took to the streets ostensibly to protest Israel. Yet the demonstrators shouted, in Arabic, "We will shoot the Jews" and called for an intifada in the city. Perhaps they took some comfort in the views of Ilmar Reepalu, who was mayor of the city from 1994 to 2013. He was known to Jews throughout the world for saying things like "Malmö does not accept anti-Semitism and does not accept Zionism," and the city's Jews "have the possibility to affect the way they are seen by society," as if they are to blame for the hatred directed against them.

The reality is ugly, yet no one wants to face it. No one, that is, except far right parties, who happily leap into the chasm to demonize Muslims and stoke xenophobia for their own political gain. As Alain Finkielkraut has put it: The reason Marine Le Pen is successful is because "there actually is a problem of Islam in France, and until now she has been the only one to dare say it."

The cycle is clear and quite dangerous: An Islamist does something terrible. Left-wing politicians and the liberal press ignore it, to the extent that they can, or find a way to excuse it as the result of poverty or disempowerment or bad politics or some other failure of the democracy. Meantime, right-wing parties exploit it relentlessly—and see their poll numbers rise. The beginning and the end of this cycle are both terrible for a country's Jews.

What was so notable about this year's German intelligence report on Islamist anti-Semitism is that it was the first official report of its kind *in all of Europe*. France stopped categorizing who carried out anti-Semitic attacks in 2011. And even the way Germany itself counts is deeply flawed, almost as if the government is intent on keeping the facts hazy. James Angelos noted in his exhaustive May 2019 *New York Times Magazine* piece about "the new German anti-Semitism" that when the perpetrator of an attack was unknown, it was automatically classified as right-wing, thus the official statistic that 89 percent of attacks were carried out by those on the far right. Yet in a 2018 European Union survey, more than half of the German Jews questioned said they had experienced anti-Semitic harassment and 41 percent of them believed that the perpetrator of the worst harassment was "someone with a Muslim extremist view."

In Sweden, the nature of the threat is routinely denied. In a powerful op-ed for *The New York Times* in 2017, "The Uncomfortable Truth About Swedish Anti-Semitism," the Swedish writer Paulina Neuding noted: "Two years ago, Sweden's biggest newspaper, *Aftonbladet*, published a column that ridiculed the notion that Jews were talking of leaving the country because of anti-Semitism, dismissing it as 'lying' and 'hysteria,' and scoffing at the 'especially cool' machine guns that police officers use when protecting Jewish schools. The same newspaper accused Israel of harvesting Palestinian organs in 2009—the modern equivalent of the blood libel."

These countries and their authorities do not just turn a blind eye to anti-Semitism. In perhaps the most disturbing case of the past two decades, at least 1,500 girls and boys were groomed, trafficked, and raped by a group of Islamist men, many of Pakistani origin, in the British town of Rotherham. But fear of being accused of bigotry prevented the police, not to mention multiple social workers, from acting on information they'd been aware of for years. More recently in Belgium, prosecutors dismissed a discrimination complaint filed against a Turkish café owner who had posted a sign saying that dogs were welcome in his café "but Jews are not." I fail to see how this doesn't qualify as discrimination—and anti-Semitism—of the crudest kind.

In a way, this denial of danger is nothing new for Europe. Think back to the 1972 Munich Olympics, and the circumstances that led to the brutal murder of eleven Israelis at the games. Those athletes and coaches were left exposed because Germany was intent on showing the world that it had transformed, that Hitler's country, which hosted the 1936 Games in Berlin, was dead and buried. So at the height of the Cold War, the guards at the Olympic Village were armed only with walkie-talkies. When eight Palestinian terrorists from Black September set out to take the Israelis hostage, all they had to do was climb a six-foot chain-link fence. In the end, Germany's worst fear was fulfilled: Eleven Jews murdered again in the country that produced the Holocaust. Yet again, Jews were killed because a society had told itself an extravagant lie.

. . .

It is hard to overstate the failure of those who claim to be the biggest defenders of liberal values—the journalists, intellectuals, commentators, professors, feminists, gay rights activists, and so on—on this score. They who have so much to say about gender equality and gay rights and due process and religious tolerance and freedom of the press and of conscience are suspiciously mum when it comes to the clear and present danger radical Islam poses to those values. In Europe they are afraid of something more immediate: "For fear of not setting one community against another, you wind up hiding things," the French philosopher Pascal Bruckner has said. Americans have even less of an excuse.

When Western intellectuals do weigh in, it is often to apologize or to justify or even to inadvertently regurgitate an Islamist talking point. The corruption of this class is brilliantly summarized in *The Flight of the Intellectuals*, in which Paul Berman shows how some of our leading lights embraced the Islamist thinker Tariq Ramadan while eschewing Ayaan Hirsi Ali.

Their grave error is in thinking, somehow, that the violence is deserved. That Islamism is somehow revenge or payback or just deserts for American imperialism or bad Israeli policy or even Israel's very existence. That anything Western or American is oppressive and bad and guaranteed to cause harm, while anything of the third world or Islamic is somehow beyond reproach.

This is the logic that led the archbishop of Canterbury, Robert Runcie; Jimmy Carter; and legions of gilded names to say, variously, that Salman Rushdie's fatwa was somehow self-inflicted, that Islamic-inspired blasphemy laws should be extended in the West in the name of tolerance, and that *The Satanic Verses* should never have been published. The United Kingdom's chief rabbi, Lord Immanuel Jakobovits, shamefully added his voice to suggest that Rushdie "abused freedom of speech." (For a more exhaustive treatment of this episode, see Deborah Lipstadt's book *Antisemitism Here and Now.*)

This is the same logic that framed the *Charlie Hebdo* attacks as somehow deserved because the cartoons incited the terrorists to come into the offices of a satirical newspaper to shoot twelve people for the sin of drawing. One wonders what, exactly, the Jews shopping at the kosher Hyper Cacher market before Shabbat did to incite their murders that afternoon in January 2015.

Those looking for a nonideological explanation for Islamist terror continue to insist that people turn to terror when they are poor or uneducated or disenfranchised, but the data has shown definitively that this is not the case. On average, Islamist terrorists are more educated and wealthier than their neighbors, like the nine who massacred more than 250 Christians on Easter 2019 in

Sri Lanka. It seems that the notion that people are actually motivated by the ideas they say they are motivated by is too difficult to bear. And so other explanations are called up: politics, economics, and so on.

That such a vanishingly small number of American intellectuals are willing to talk honestly about this proves the very thing they are pretending isn't true: that Islamist violence, which begins by tagging a person as an enemy of Islam or an Islamophobe, is deserving of fear. And they are right to assume that they will be smeared, because there is a cottage industry of advocacy groups and nonprofits who do just that. The Southern Poverty Law Center, for decades an admirable organization that fought groups like the KKK, began its downward descent into ignominy when it designated my friend Maajid Nawaz as an "anti-Muslim extremist." This was a truly rich description given that Nawaz is a former Islamist who was jailed in Egypt for four years for his work as a jihadi recruiter and who today does anti-extremist work rehabilitating former Islamists through his nonprofit organization, Quilliam. He sued for defamation and won more than $3 million, but the reputational damage was done. When I bring up the name of this liberal Muslim who is fighting for the values liberals claim to cherish, too often those same liberals make a face as if they've smelled spoiled milk.

"We used to have a zillion writers on the topic of communism," writer Paul Berman said in an interview with Tunku Varadarajan in *The Daily Beast.* "It was a perfectly normal thing for American intellectuals to weigh in on the debate over the Soviet Union, and the Cold War. But it's not normal for people to weigh in on debates on Islam." So what explains the change? "People are mostly concerned that they're not seen as Islamophobes. And if your principal concern is to show that you're not Islamophobe, one way to guarantee that is to say not one word on the subject! Besides, people are frightened by a million things: They're frightened by the topic, by the controversy that surrounds the topic, and obviously there's a degree of physical intimidation that goes with this. There are, in fact, topics that no one in his right mind is going to take up for reasons of physical fear."

This goes a long way toward explaining why these sorts of people will harp endlessly about a bakery that won't make a gay wedding cake but have nothing to say about honor killings. It goes a long way toward explaining why those who leave fundamentalist Christianity, like Megan Phelps-Roper, are cheered, while those who leave Islam, like the equally admirable Sarah Haider, are shunned.

There are costs to being too willing to give in to a dangerous, even racist, moral relativism; for being too cowardly to say that not all cultures are equally good at protecting women, gays, and religious minorities; for being too close-minded to see that the motivation here is primarily ideological and not material. The cost is that those who remain silent are making the implicit case that the violence and the anti-Semitism that originate from this source are somehow politically legitimate.

．．．

In America, contrary to what the president would have you believe, caravans of Middle Eastern terrorists are not crossing our southern border. And Muslims in America report feeling pride in being American and a sense of optimism about the future, despite being routine targets of dehumanization on the part of this administration, its Republican enablers, and its allies on Fox.

Though the Census Bureau does not collect information on Americans' religious identities, by all reasonable estimates there are some 3.5 million Muslim Americans. And most of them (58 percent) are first-generation Americans, hailing from countries all over the world. A 2017 Pew poll found that 92 percent of Muslims in America say they are proud to be American. They have also retained their particular identity: 97 percent report being proud Muslims. And four of five American Muslims (80 percent) report being "satisfied with the way things are going in their lives."

That doesn't mean there hasn't been violence. In 2006, a Muslim American who expressed hatred of Israel shot six people, killing one of them, at the Jewish Federation of Greater Seattle. Four Muslim men were arrested in a plot to bomb two Bronx synagogues in 2009. A Muslim convert was thwarted by the FBI in his plan to blow up a Florida synagogue in 2016. In 2018, Mohamed Abdi Mohamed, a Somali immigrant, shouted anti-Semitic slurs while aiming his car at people leaving a Los Angeles synagogue.

The number of troubling incidents is growing. Just consider the month of May 2019. Early in the month, a video surfaced from an April event at the Muslim American Society in Philadelphia in which children were filmed singing, "We will chop off their heads, and we will liberate the sorrowful and exalted Al-Aqsa Mosque. We will lead the army of Allah fulfilling his promise, and we will subject them to eternal torture." In the middle of the month, Rabab Abdulhadi, an Arab and Muslim ethnicities studies professor at San Francisco State University, gave a mandatory lecture to an anthropology class in which she reportedly said that anyone who supports Israel is a white supremacist. On May 16, Ali Kourani was convicted of working for Hezbollah's Islamic Jihad to help the terrorist group plan and carry out attacks in the United States. According to the U.S. attorney, "Kourani's chilling mission was to help procure weapons and gather intelligence about potential targets in the U.S. for future Hezbollah terrorist attacks. Some of the targets Kourani surveilled included JFK Airport and law enforcement facilities in New York City, including the federal building at 26 Federal Plaza in Manhattan." The case led the U.S. National Counterterrorism Center to come to the chilling conclusion that "Hezbollah is determined to give itself a potential homeland option as a critical component of its terrorism playbook." On May 19, an Uber driver threw two women out of his car when he learned he was driving them from an Israel Independence Day event, saying he was a Palestinian. On May 22, a twenty-year-old named Jonathan Xie was arrested for offering material support to Hamas and for threatening, in an Instagram video with a gun and a Hamas flag, to "shoot the pro-Israel demonstrators."

The conspiracy theories that propelled nineteen Islamists to hijack those four airplanes and murder 2,977 Americans are the same ones that motivated Xie to threaten Jews from his New Jersey home. Thankfully, the FBI caught him before he could do real damage. The bureau did the same in June when it foiled another attack, this one a church bombing in Pittsburgh that Mustafa Mousab Alowemer, a twenty-one-year-old refugee from Daraa, Syria, was allegedly planning to carry out in the name of ISIS.

What the FBI cannot stop is the spread of a worldview that soft-pedals or justifies Islamist violence and, in so doing, ultimately soft-pedals or justifies anti-Semitism as an expression of legitimate political grievance. This ideology is a direct threat not just to Jews but to America. And you can see the ways in which it has started to seep into the Democratic Party.

You could see hints of it when, in 2009, Homeland Security secretary Janet Napolitano refused to use the word "terrorism," instead relying on the unforgettable euphemism "man-caused disasters." You could see it when President Obama, in an interview with Vox following the *Charlie Hebdo* and Hyper Cacher supermarket killings, said, "My first job is to protect the American people. It is entirely legitimate for the American people to be deeply concerned when you've got a bunch of violent, vicious zealots who behead people or randomly shoot a bunch of folks in a deli in Paris." But of course these incidents were not random. The supermarket was selected by the killers because it was kosher. Rather than apologize for the gaffe, the administration dug in deeper. "There were not all victims of one background or one nationality," Jen Psaki, a State Department spokesman, said. In fact, they were. But that didn't stop White House press secretary Josh Earnest from insisting to ABC's Jonathan Karl, when pressed about the president's use of the word "random," that "there were people other than just Jews who were in that deli."

It is hard not to think back to the official French response, at least initially, to the Ilan Halimi murder, which went to great lengths to insist on its randomness. Later, the Obama administration walked all of this back, but I still hear Jews making sardonic jokes about how they are the "randomly chosen people."

You can see it when, in 2015, John Kerry responded to a question from *The Atlantic*'s Jeffrey Goldberg about the genocidal anti-Semitism of the Iranian regime this way: "I think they have a fundamental ideological confrontation with Israel at this particular moment. Whether or not that translates into active steps to, quote, 'Wipe it,' you know . . ."

Does it sound like a debate about Israel's borders or settlements when Ayatollah Ali Khamenei said, in 2001: "It is the mission of the Islamic Republic of Iran to erase Israel from the map of the region"? Does this, uttered by Hossein Salami, the deputy head of the Revolutionary Guard in 2014, sound like an "ideological confrontation" confined to a "particular moment": "Today we are aware of how the Zionist regime is slowly being erased from the world, and indeed, soon, there will be no such thing as the Zionist regime on Planet Earth"? No, this sounds like a twenty-first-century Hitler—and one on the brink of getting nuclear weapons.

You see it when California progressives put forward a resolution before the state party convention in which they place some of the blame for the Pittsburgh massacre on . . . Israel. The massacre, according to the draft resolution, was "the culmination of an alarming re-emergence of virulent antisemitism that is a core element of historical and currently resurgent white supremacism in the United States and around the world." Okay: so far, so reasonable. Then it continued: the "Israeli government, along with some of its U.S. backers, welcomed support from Christian fundamentalist and ultra-right groups in the United States and abroad, dangerously ignoring their deeply rooted antisemitism while aligning with their virulent Islamophobia." Such logic may pass muster in Jeremy Corbyn's Labour Party, but until very recently it was absolute anathema in the United States.

No recent political story better exemplifies how these troubling ideological trends have moved from the disreputable to the respectable than the way the Democratic Party has rallied around the now-famous freshman congresswoman from Minnesota, Ilhan Omar. Omar has a life story that anyone with a heart would be moved by. She is a refugee from Somalia. A religious Muslim who wears a hijab, she is one of the first Muslims to be elected to Congress, and the first woman of color to represent Minnesota in Congress. It's no wonder that *Time* magazine put her on the cover, that Annie Leibovitz snapped her picture, and that she makes every important women-to-watch list.

For months, all of this understandable celebration of her identity overshadowed her ideas. They were there, for anyone to see, but few wanted to look. So in January 2019 I wrote about some of her most troubling views in a *New York Times* column called "Ilhan Omar and the Myth of Jewish Hypnosis."

By now you know that the conspiracy theory of the Jew as the hypnotic conspirator and the sinister manipulator is one with ancient roots and a bloody history. Thus it did not bode well that in 2012, during one of Israel's periodic wars with Hamas in Gaza, Ilhan Omar, at the time a nutrition coordinator with the Minnesota Department of Education, tweeted the following: "Israel has hypnotized the world, may Allah awaken the people and help them see the evil doings of Israel. #Gaza #Palestine #Israel." Rather than apologize, forthrightly and strongly, when asked on CNN in January 2019 what she had to say to "Jewish Americans who find that deeply offensive," Omar responded, "That's a really regrettable way of expressing that," speaking not of her tweet but of the way the anchor, Poppy Harlow, phrased the question. "I don't know how my comments would be offensive to Jewish Americans," Omar continued. "My comments precisely are addressing what was happening during the Gaza War and I'm clearly speaking about the way the Israeli regime was conducting itself in that war."

Shortly thereafter, in February, Omar, by way of criticizing America's support of Israel, tweeted, "It's all about the Benjamins baby." When an editor at the Jewish newspaper *The Forward* asked what she meant, she replied: "AIPAC!" Then, in March, Omar gave a speech in which she described 9/11 as an event in which "some people did something." She delivered the speech to the Council on American-Islamic Relations, a group founded by leaders of the Islamic Association for Palestine, a Hamas-affiliated anti-Semitic propaganda organization.

For a brief period, Omar took a lot of heat in the press. But soon enough the media scrum moved on to the next Trump scandal and many in her party stood by her side. Their defenses became even more full-throated—Bernie

Sanders called her "a leader with strength and courage"—after President Trump shared an incendiary video on Twitter in which Omar played down the 9/11 attacks.

These days, Omar remains on the House Foreign Affairs Committee. The former Obama staffers who host the hugely popular podcast *Pod Save America* welcomed her on. Stephen Colbert brought her on his show in April 2019. Of the various Democrats who rallied to her cause, Representative Jim Clyburn's comments were particularly memorable. Omar is "living through a lot of pain," Clyburn, the third-highest-ranking Democrat in the House, said. "I'm serious about that. There are people who tell me, 'Well, my parents are Holocaust survivors.' 'My parents did this.' It's more personal with her."

Every political party has fringe figures. Generally, such figures are either marginalized or ignored. But here it seemed that something had shifted. It wasn't enough to ignore or censure Omar while also criticizing the president for his vile fixation on her. She had to be vociferously defended, and her comments had to be contextualized or otherwise explained away.

The fact that the most powerful figures in the Democratic Party and their allies in the press have decided that Omar is worth defending, is worth the tremendous political capital being spent on her, should wake everyone up to where the party could be heading. What the Democrats have already made clear is that saying bigoted things about Jews has become entirely politically survivable.

L'affaire Omar was a signal event; there will be many

more like it to come. The theme will be the same: ignoring or forgiving anti-Semitism for the sake of the people espousing it, which is in fact a profound insult to those people. It is to champion people simply for being outsiders while denying those key aspects of American culture that have always allowed outsiders to become insiders.

Just as early Americans had to disavow their loyalty to a foreign king, giving up your anti-Semitism is a condition of adapting to America. The country could not function with royalists, and it cannot survive if anti-Semites are in positions of power. Both things are inimical to our liberal democracy.

CHAPTER 6

HOW TO FIGHT

During college, the required reading included *The Republic* and the New Testament; Burke and Nietzsche; Virginia Woolf and *The Souls of Black Folk*. All stuck with me. But the essay that changed my life in the most personal way was a short piece located on a long-abandoned website that was down more often that it was functional.

"How to Fight Anti-Semitism" was written by a Columbia alumnus named Ze'ev Maghen, who had been a student in the early 1990s. Maghen was responding to what has now become a regular feature of campus life: a known anti-Semite invited to give a speech on an elite campus. This particular address was delivered by one Leonard Jeffries, then the chairman of City College of New York's African American studies department. Mr. Jeffries had said, "Everyone knows rich Jews helped finance the slave trade." He also believed that "the Jews" controlled Hollywood and were part of a larger genocidal plot. "Russian Jewry," he declared in a 1991 speech at the Empire State Black Arts and Cultural Festival in Albany, "had a particular control over the monies, and their financial partners, the Mafia, put together a system for the destruction of black people. It was by design."

Needless to say, the Jewish community at Columbia was not thrilled that such a man would be honored with a podium at the university. I had the same feeling, years later, when my alma mater offered the biggest venue on campus to Iran's Mahmoud Ahmadinejad, an anti-Semite with considerably more power than Jeffries.

In Maghen's time, the Jewish community on campus organized a protest similar to pretty much every organized American Jewish communal protest I've ever seen. It was reactive and defensive, the protestors almost pleading with onlookers to verify their fundamental humanity. Maghen was outraged by the fundamental weakness of such an approach. "A man calls you a pig," he wrote. "Do you walk around with a sign explaining that, in fact, you are *not* a pig? Do you hand out leaflets expostulating in detail upon the manifold differences between you and a pig?"

How many times had I succumbed to exactly this logic? How much time had I wasted cajoling, trying to convince people who thought I was nothing more than an animal that I was a person just like them? "Did you really think you could *protest* anti-Semitism away?" he asked. "Did you honestly believe that rally number seven-hundred-fifty-six-thousand-four-hundred-and-twenty-three was going to produce results all its predecessors, in America, Europe and elsewhere, consistently have not?"

Yes! I had! I had thought exactly that without acknowledging it. The depth of my mistake shocked me awake.

"Ask yourself," Maghen wrote, and the question felt directed right at me,

> why are we still here? What is the key to our unique, defiant, unparalleled survival against all odds and forecasts? St. Paul predicted we'd "wither away," Hegel said our jig was up, Spengler consigned us to "winter season," Toynbee called us a fossil. Wrong, gentlemen. So what is it, this ingredient that makes us the "Indestructible Jews?" What, as Mark Twain asks, is the secret of our immortality? Surely none of you will tell me that down four millennia, and through the wrenching vicissitudes and savage depredations of exile, it was our appeals, protests and screams for equitable treatment that sustained us, kept us in life, and brought us to this season. No, my friends, our history teaches us a different lesson: that those who, rather than appealing and screaming, choose to build, to educate toward cultural and national revival, to defy anti-Semitism not with Jewish pleas and Jewish hand-wringing but with Jewish learning, Jewish observance, Jewish strength and Jewish achievement—such are those who bring our people survival, salvation, a future.

I suddenly saw all of the debates and hand-wringing inside the Jewish community about the latest boycott of Israeli hummus at the local food co-op, or the right response to Israeli Apartheid Week, or the proper approach to the appearance of a swastika on campus—a silent protest? a strongly worded press release? a dialogue group?—as not just a waste of our precious time but a betrayal of what we were meant to do and be. I began to realize that building was better than begging, affirming better than adjuring. Not just better strategically, but better for Jews emotionally and intellectually and spiritually.

"Non-Jews respect Jews who respect Judaism, and they are embarrassed by Jews who are embarrassed by Judaism," Rabbi Jonathan Sacks has said, riffing on the key theme of the late Lubavitcher rebbe, who built the Chabad movement. What is more attractive than people confident in themselves, grateful for their historical legacy, and proud of their culture?

Maghen's essay does not provide the whole answer, but it fundamentally reoriented my posture. It moved me from crouching to standing, from defense to offense, from doubt to confidence, from shame to pride.

Nothing can remind you of who you are like a gut punch. It is natural and healthy to push back against the bully. But if the response ends there, with anger, you have missed a tremendous opportunity to examine *why* you wanted to fight back and *what*, exactly, you wanted to fight for.

I have tried in the previous pages to describe, as honestly and plainly as I am able, the nature of this three-headed dragon so that Americans of all faiths and creeds can see it and confront it. But just as I hope it will be clear that the "how to fight" structure of this chapter is part of the larger "how to fight" spirit of this book, I hope that when I speak as a Jew addressing other Jews about the burdens and obligations of this urgent moment, and about the American and Jewish pride that I feel, readers will hear in my words a call that is meant for them. That is meant for you.

There has not been a single moment in Jewish history in which there weren't anti-Semites determined to eradicate Judaism and the Jews. But the Jews did not sustain their magnificent civilization because they were anti-anti-Semites. They sustained it because they knew who they were and *why* they were. They were lit up not by fires from without but by the fires in their souls.

Likewise, we fight by waging an affirmative battle *for* who we are. By entering the fray for our values, for our ideas, for our ancestors, for our families, for our communities, for the generations that will come after us.

Just as there is a three-headed dragon—the far right, the far left, and radical Islam—I believe there are also three key ways to think about how to fight this beast. One is how we orient ourselves toward our enemies. The second is how we orient ourselves toward our allies. And the third, and most important, is how we orient ourselves toward ourselves.

The fight begins with what I have tried hard to do in this book:

Tell the truth.

This sounds simple, but it may be the hardest rule to follow. Sometimes we tell ourselves lies because reality is too painful to face.

One such inconvenient truth is that, at least for the time being, Jews in countries like Hungary and Poland, which are governed by fascist-adjacent leaders who promote ethnic nationalism, report feeling far safer (by a twenty-point margin) than Jews in countries like France and Germany, countries that have done much more to welcome refugees and migrants. This fact undermines something American Jews, given recent European history, tend to believe with religious fervency: that ethnic nationalism always puts us in grave danger and liberal democracies always protect us.

History makes me certain that the status quo for the Jews in Hungary and Poland will not last. Political systems that are ruled by the whim of one man never end up protecting Jews. "The best bulwark against Islamists is not the far right. It is democracy," as Francis Kalifat, the president of the French Jewish communal organization CRIF, told *The Wall Street Journal*.

I do not believe that turning away from the values that have always saved us—the rule of law, tolerance of difference, a shared civic culture—is in any way the solution, nor do I pretend to have the answers to the knotty problem of cultural balkanization in Europe. But I do think that to see our way through this difficult pass, we have to be honest about it.

Trust your discomfort.

We Jews have a reputation for anxiety and hysteria, but Larry David aside, most of us actually underplay the discomfort we deal with, eager to put on a good face, to blend in with our neighbors, keen not to play the victim.

This rule is a simple one: Don't wait. If an organization you supported is making common cause with Louis Farrakhan, do not look for a way to justify their relationship with a man who has insisted, "Here the Jews don't like Farrakhan and so they call me 'Hitler.' Well, that's a good name. Hitler was a very great man." If a politician you thought represented your values claims that Israel is among the worst abusers of human rights in the world, you now know the truth about that politician.

This June, when the Cambridge Student Union hosted the Malaysian prime minister, a proud anti-Semite and Holocaust denier who recently described Jews as "hooknosed," he told the audience: "I have some Jewish friends, very good friends. They are not like the other Jews, that's why they are my friends." The vile comment did not inspire a mass walkout but elicited laughs from the audience—a room full of some of the most educated people on the planet. I admit that I had to watch the video several times to make sure I had seen and heard what I had seen and heard, so painful was it to admit. But my eyes and ears were not lying. Neither are yours.

Call it out. Especially when it's hard.

When a right-wing person attacks us, it is a relief. In the circles American Jews tend to travel in, calling out politicians like Steve King is easy. Calling out Ilhan Omar is not. That is because Omar is herself targeted by racists and lunatics who wish her harm because of her faith, her gender, or the color of her skin.

Two things can be true at once: Ilhan Omar can espouse bigoted ideas. And Ilhan Omar can herself be the hate object of bigots, including the president of the United States.

Yet many people seem unable to hold both of these truths in their heads at the same time. If you criticize Omar's anti-Semitism you may be called hysterical or oversensitive. More likely, you will be called a racist, a white supremacist, or a fascist who is actively endangering the life of a minority—a purposeful tactic used to make a person who holds bad ideas above reproach.

No one wants to be accused of such things. And no one wants to ruin a dinner party or to lose friends or to seem parochial. And so what I see too often among friends is that they keep their mouths shut and hope someone changes the subject. As my friend David Samuels has said: American Jews are eager to be the right kind of victims—meaning victims of the bad people on the right, and not the good people on the left. The upshot is that there is a conspiracy of silence taking hold among too many progressive Jews. Outrage is increasingly reserved for the privacy and safety of our own homes.

This tactic will not stop the spread of anti-Semitism. It will hasten it. So speak out soberly and responsibly by criticizing ideas, not identities. Doing so will probably make your life a bit less comfortable. But since when is being a fun guest at a dinner party more important than standing up for what matters?

Apply the kippah (or Magen David) test.

In the first three decades of my life, I never wore a Magen David necklace. It always seemed redundant to me. But since the Pittsburgh attack, I have worn a Jewish star pendant regularly, especially in public venues and in situations where I am conscious of being one of the only Jews in the room. This show of pride has become important to me. I want people to know that I am unafraid.

This is the example set by Mitchell Leshchiner during his middle school graduation this Spring in Vernon Hills, Illinois. Leshchiner doesn't usually wear a kippah. But the Poway shooting changed things for the fourteen-year-old. "It was important to make a statement that we're still here, and that no matter what happens, we'll still be here," he said.

When I started traveling the country to give talks

about how to respond to this moment, I asked others to do the same. The only way to fight anti-Semitism, I urged after Pittsburgh, was to never cower in the face of fear.

But I have to confess that this full-throated advice has lately felt too simplistic, too unaware of the various contexts Jews might find themselves in. My friend Jamie and his boyfriend were recently walking to a wedding in Berlin wearing kippot and they were spit on. Would it have been better if they weren't wearing them that day? Or was there something character-building about the experience? I am not a parent, but when I ask parents if they would allow their child to take the risk, the almost universal impulse is to protect the child's safety.

You know your community better than I do. In Pittsburgh or New York, I would never hesitate to wear a Magen David. In Paris or Berlin, I hope I would make the same choice, but I am not sure.

Some exceptional people will always run toward the fire. People like the late Dr. Jerry Rabinowitz of Pittsburgh. Or people like Almog Peretz, a veteran of the Israel Defense Forces, who, in Poway, ran to help get the children out of harm's way and took a bullet in the leg, or like Oscar Stewart, who rushed the killer. But most people are not wired that way.

So my advice is this: Ask yourself if where you are living passes the kippah test. If you would be uncomfortable wearing a kippah or a Magen David necklace in your neighborhood, you should make a plan to improve your neighborhood or make a plan to leave it.

More than half (55 percent) of all French Jews have considered emigrating over the past year. And no wonder. It is not a good sign that many are leaving rural towns and villages to move to the few neighborhoods that remain safe for Jews in Paris. They call it "internal exile." Meantime, nearly 40 percent of British Jews say they will "seriously consider emigrating" if Jeremy Corbyn becomes prime minister, according to a *Jewish Chronicle* poll.

Ask yourself: Can I safely assert my Jewishness where I live?

And if you do find yourself being spit on or cursed at, remember: You are part of a noble tradition of people others have long tried to humiliate for standing up for the true and the good. In time, the ones being shamed will be the ones venerated as heroes.

Don't trust people who seek to divide Jews. Even if they are Jews.

We've seen that the world has often tried to separate the "good" Jews from the "bad" ones. What may be a surprise is the equally long history of Jews doing the same.

Menelaus was a high priest who worked in the Temple under the Greeks during the time of the Maccabees. Other high priests had tried to accommodate the Greeks with bribes, but Menelaus went all in. He put statues of Zeus in the Temple and convinced Antiochus to force the Jews to Hellenize their rituals. Otto Weininger was the

Jewish German philosopher who converted to Christianity and whose ideas of Judaism as "the extreme of cowardliness" and Jewishness as pathetic femininity were taken up by the Nazis. Stella Kübler was the Aryan-looking German Jew who actively collaborated with the Gestapo as a *Greiferin,* a "catcher" of Berlin's Jews who were trying to pass as Aryan.

There have long been multiple intentions and motives for Jews to betray one another. Often people did it in times of lethal danger, thinking they would save themselves or even others if they accommodated to power. Some people did it because they were craven. But ultimately they all undermined the safety and security of actual Jews. Anyone who participates in this ugly work— I think of the small cohort of anti-Zionist Jews who insist that the only real Jews are the ones who disavow the State of Israel—is doing to themselves what Farrakhan does to us: insisting on separating out the good Jews from the "Satanic ones."

Allow for the possibility of change.

When Hugo Black was nominated to join the Supreme Court, the *Pittsburgh Post-Gazette* revealed that he had been involved in the KKK. To make matters worse, Black defended himself with the classic lines: "I number among my friends many members of the colored race" and "Some of my best and most intimate friends are Catholics and Jews."

The idea that a man with this history would be one of the country's most powerful people was profane. But Black became one of the great justices of the twentieth century, a mainstay of the Warren Court and a vocal champion of *Brown v. Board of Education.* People can change.

I think also of Derek Black, the godson of David Duke and the actual son of the man who started Stormfront, the first popular white supremacist website. Black was once a rising star in that bigoted world. Today he fights against it.

And I think perhaps most of Mohammed Dajani, whose life story is proof that we are not condemned to the circumstances of our birth. Born in 1946, Dajani grew up in Jerusalem, in an environment in which every time he'd fight with his brother, as he told David Horovitz of *The Times of Israel,* his grandmother would say, "Goddamn the Jews, the Jews are responsible for us two kids fighting." He spent years as a political radical and a committed anti-Semite, eventually becoming a senior Fatah operative.

The turning point came, as it often does, in a hospital. In Israel, hospitals like Jerusalem's Hadassah Ein Kerem, are islands of coexistence between Israelis and Palestinians, and it was there that Dajani's father was getting cancer treatments. "To my shock, I started to observe that the doctors and the nurses treated him as a patient," he told Horovitz. Witnessing the kindness, he recalled, "awakened my humanity. This was the starting point."

Ultimately, that awakening would lead him to bring the first organized group of Palestinian students to Auschwitz in 2014. The trip destroyed Dajani's career: He was fired from his professorship at Al-Quds University, smeared as a collaborator, his life threatened. According to Dajani, the school even threw out every one of the thousands of books he'd donated to the library. "I don't worry about who is following," he says. "I think that the message is more important—carry it and keep standing up for it."

Change is always possible; it is never too late. The ending of any given story has not been written.

Notice your enemies. But even more, notice your friends.

It's painful to be torn apart publicly, especially when those you believed were your friends join in or remain on the sidelines, scared to speak up and catch flak. Perhaps more painful than the nasty things some people say is the silence of those you thought were your allies.

But one thousand voices condemning you—even ten thousand—will be, I promise you, drowned out when a single person you admire tells you that you are courageous, that you are standing up for what's right, that you've inspired them to do the same. Make sure you are listening closely for the single voice that will mean more to you than the braying mob. Pay it forward by being that voice for someone else.

Follow the Pittsburgh principle.

It may sound strange, but the reaction to Pittsburgh gave me a tremendous amount of hope that we are not alone in this fight. As one of my rabbis, Danny Schiff, has pointed out, at first glance what happened in Pittsburgh was yet another pogrom among the countless pogroms our people have suffered. But take a closer look.

On November 9, 1938, when the Nazis set fire to hundreds of synagogues throughout Germany on Kristallnacht, ordinary Germans joined in or stood by to watch the fires burn. In Pittsburgh, the reaction was the opposite. The entire community—Muslim leaders, Christian leaders, politicians, government leaders, police departments, corporations, even our sports teams—stood up and said no. We will not give this oxygen.

Too often when the Jewish people were set upon, the authorities and the surrounding community abetted the attack. This is still, tragically, the case in much of Europe; too many non-Jewish Europeans somehow still do not see an attack on Jews as an attack on themselves. (Think back to the Raymond Barre gaffe about the killing of Jews versus "innocent Frenchmen.")

This is what makes America so different. Non-Jewish Americans understood that an attack on the Jewish community was an attack on them, too. As Wasi Mohamed, then the head of the Islamic Center of Pittsburgh, pointed out: "Negative rhetoric against the Jewish community is poison. You know, it's poison for our democracy, it's poison for our country, and it's negative to everybody, not just that community."

Mohamed's support—not to mention that of the Pittsburgh Steelers; numerous people from the organization showed up at the funeral of Cecil and David Rosenthal, with a former defensive lineman, Brett Keisel, serving as pallbearer—wasn't a favor bestowed on us. These neighbors were coming forward to defend their values as well.

This is a departure from history that cannot be understated. "This breathtaking and profoundly moving reality is virtually unparalleled in the Jewish experience," Rabbi Schiff wrote in *The Washington Post*. "It demands a reappraisal of the classic anti-Semitism narrative. Once, in the not so distant past, Jews faced evil essentially alone; now, whatever evil Jews face in the United States is vastly overmatched by a sea of goodness."

Pittsburgh can be a model not just for the rest of the country, but for the rest of the diaspora. Crucially, the test here is not a test of the Jews. It is a test of our surrounding societies. As one of my mentors, Jonathan Rosen, wrote in *The New York Times* in 2001: "When the Jews of Europe were murdered in the Holocaust, one might have concluded that European Judaism failed—to defend itself, to anticipate evil, to make itself acceptable to the world around it, to pack up and leave. But one could also conclude in a deeper way that Christian Europe failed—to accept the existence of Jews in their midst, and it has been marked ever since, and will be for all time, with this blot on its culture. Israel is a test of its neighbors as much as its neighbors are a test for Israel. If the Israeli experiment fails, then Islam will have failed, and so will the Christian culture that plays a shaping role in that part of the region."

Who will pass the test?

Praise those who do the right thing.

In May, the German Bundestag declared that "the pattern of argument and the methods of BDS are anti-Semitic" and—more—that they are "clearly reminiscent of Nazi-era anti-Jewish boycotts." This was a righteous stance, and one that, at least it seemed to me, went mostly unnoticed.

Have you heard of the Kreuzberg Initiative Against Anti-Semitism? I am embarrassed to admit that I hadn't until I began working on this book. It is an organization in Berlin that works to fight anti-Semitism, particularly in Muslim communities. That it was founded by a group of Muslims makes it all the more remarkable. Also remarkable are heroes like Rachel Riley, the famous British television host who uses her platform to relentlessly expose the anti-Semitism of the Labour Party, and courageous whistleblowers like Louise Withers Green and Sam Matthews.

Rabbis across the country should be using their sermons to make heroes of such groups and people. We want to make it easier for others to do the right thing.

At the same time, we must fight the anti-Semitism on our own side.

As the brilliant Rabbi Angela Warnick Buchdahl of Central Synagogue in Manhattan put it in her 2018 Rosh Hashanah sermon, which she devoted to the rise of anti-Semitism: "Be honest: Were you more outraged that Tamika Mallory refused to denounce Farrakhan, or were you more outraged by Trump's inability to flatly denounce the white supremacists after Charlottesville? Are you making excuses for one of them?

"In order to be principled in this fight, we must be willing to call out the anti-Semitism on our *own side of the aisle*," she said. "It's easy to convince ourselves that the one on 'our side' exists only at the powerless fringe, or that it's outweighed by more important ideological alliances. But we have to be as intolerant of anti-Semitism from our political allies as from our foes."

That is exactly what my friends Carly Pildis, a long-time progressive organizer, and Amanda Berman, who runs a progressive Zionist organization called Zioness, have modeled. After the 2019 Dyke March in Washington, D.C., announced that Jewish pride flags would be banned, Pildis and Berman showed up on a day's notice with a group of other allies to support those queer Jewish women who wanted to march with their flags. Watching from afar, I feared that the whole thing would be fruit-less. But showing up led to success: The parade marshals ultimately allowed the Jewish women—and their flags—into the event.

Their experience offers two instructive lessons. First is the power of showing up. "The people complaining about the bigotry on the left who think 'someone else will deal with this, I'd rather go to brunch' are either lazy or not seeing the big picture," Berman wrote me. "There is a concerted effort to push Jews out of these spaces and then point to the fact that we aren't there. We have to be there. We've always been there. And now is not the time to hope someone else represents our community." The second lesson is the power of speaking the language of the place you are in. "We weren't there to debate Israeli politics or give a treatise on Zionism," Pildis told me. "We were there to support proud queer Jewish women at their re-quest. And that's exactly what we did." Finally, by show-ing up rather than lobbing critical tweets, they gave the organizers of the march the chance to do the right thing.

What was most gratifying, said Pildis, is that multiple women said to her and Berman: "I am Jewish. I was on your side, but I was too scared to come be with you. Thank you." Once that person could have been Pildis herself. As she wrote in a piece for *Tablet* after the march: "For much of my life, I simply allowed anti-Semitism in service of the causes I cared about. I brushed it off, I swallowed my anger and continued on the march for freedom, for justice, for equity. This is a catastrophic mistake that so many of us made. I will make it no longer: If we ignore the rising tide of anti-Semitism all around us, we will all drown." Let's follow her lead.

Expect solidarity.

One of the most depressing episodes of recent months was when Felix Klein, the German government's special representative for anti-Semitism, said that because of the routine violence against visible Jews in Germany (and, for that matter, people speaking Hebrew), he could "no longer recommend Jews wear a kippah at every time and place in Germany." Klein surely was only trying to protect the country's Jewish citizens, but the impulse here was the wrong one. The right response was modeled by, of all things, a popular German tabloid called *Bild*. The paper printed a cutout kippah on the front page. "Wear it, so that your friends and neighbors can see it," the editor in chief wrote on Twitter.

This was the same spirit that drove French people to declare, *"Je suis Charlie"* and *"Je suis juif"* in the aftermath of the 2015 terrorist attacks. It was, as Bernard-Henri Lévy put it, "a reason for true hope for which we had almost stopped waiting."

Europe is very good at building memorials for dead Jews. It is still learning how to protect the living ones. Vigils honor the dead, but they don't do much for the living. Solidarity does.

Stop blaming yourself.

Many Jews seem to have an almost theological belief that anti-Semitism is somehow our fault. Maybe they believe this because it is what the world has told the Jews for so long.

Take the example of the spread of anti-Zionism. Some suggest that if Benjamin Netanyahu were not Israel's prime minister, people would abandon their belief that the State of Israel should not exist. Others argue that if anyone else were prime minister, anti-Zionism would multiply exponentially. Both ideas are as ridiculous as blaming Jews for the blood libel.

Reasonable people do not blame rape victims for their choice of dress, and reasonable people do not blame gay people for inviting anti-gay slurs, and reasonable people do not blame anti-Semitism on Jews. To think clearly about anti-Semitism, Jews must stop blaming themselves. As Ze'ev Maghen put it many years ago, we should not place ourselves in the position of beseeching our enemies to affirm that we are not, in fact, pigs. To do that, we need to truly believe that we are not.

Choose life.

These days, adhering to the most important Jewish value is not an abstraction; it can mean attending a self-defense class or an active-shooter drill or raising money for a community security assessment. Growing up, I never thought twice about my safety when I walked into a synagogue or a JCC or even a Jewish museum. Now stepping into any of those places feels like entering an airport. (Then again, going through an airport did not always feel like going through an airport until after September 11, 2001, with one exception: flying to Israel.)

At the beginning of the school year, the Manhattan Jewish preschool attended by the son of my dear friends had an unarmed guard at the door. The morning after Pittsburgh, that unarmed guard was joined by an armed one. The morning after Poway, a third guard joined the pair to stand watch every morning on the sidewalk in front of the school.

Anyone who has visited a synagogue in London or Paris or in any country in Latin America is aware that by comparison our synagogues are still wide open to the public. As Angela Merkel has said of Germany: "There is to this day not a single synagogue, not a single day-care center for Jewish children, not a single school for Jewish children that does not need to be guarded by German policemen."

Protecting Jewish lives is the job of the FBI and the police. But we can help fill the gaps. Community-led security organizations like Community Security Trust, in England, and the Jewish Community Protection Service, in France, inspired a group of Americans to create Community Security Service, an all-volunteer organization focused on training people within the Jewish community to provide professional-level security in Jewish spaces. CSS has already trained more than five thousand Jews across the country; I consistently see CSS personnel at communal events.

"It's unfortunate that we live in a time when it's necessary," Daniel Zaffran, a CSS volunteer, told me. "But we're not trying to be Chicken Little, or say the walls are closing in. I still think America is different. We have a different history. Things are under stress now, but we have faith in our government and our neighbors, and that just does not exist in most countries."

Nevertheless, we must be alert to changes in our level of comfort and be unafraid to say when we need literal protection.

Never ask of yourself what you would not ask of another minority.

I was recently at a Jewish gathering in Berkeley with a middle-aged woman who was telling me and our fellow dinner companions about a permaculture retreat she had just attended. She was gushing about the incredible diversity of the group, how there had been every kind of person: transgender folks and black folks and Latino folks and so on.

But one thing had made her slightly uncomfortable, she said after a good while. One of the people at the retreat had been telling people that the Rothschilds controlled the government. And how everyone ought to read *The Protocols of the Elders of Zion*.

This is a tragic sickness. What other group of people would experience such unrefined bigotry and lead not with the bigotry but with genuflections to the bigot's apparently sacred identity?

If you heard of a university where tenured professors regularly voiced slurs about gays, would you expect gay people to donate to that school? If a museum routinely mounted exhibits denigrating black people, would you expect black benefactors to contribute?

Do not give your time and money to causes, institutions, nonprofits, or universities that condone anti-Semitism. Is a school actually prestigious if it disparages you and the very idea of pluralism that once allowed Jews to thrive there? The question answers itself.

Resist hierarchical identity politics.

Corrupt identity politics on the right—the Olympics of Purity—tell the Jews that they can never be white or Christian enough. Corrupt identity politics on the left—the Olympics of Victimization—tell the Jews that they can never be oppressed enough. In these Manichaean views of the world, the Jews are either not white enough or they are too white. In both cases, we are framed as the enemy of "the people."

Typically, the only way out of this vise is for the Jew to confess her sins and disavow part of herself. But a political movement or party that forces us to make this choice—to check part of our identity at the door—is not one worth joining.

We should not make a deal that requires us to erase ourselves. To do so is to participate in our own slow destruction. In resisting this devil's bargain, we should follow the lead of Britain's Luciana Berger, who left Labour, the party that had been her political home for twenty years, after a vile campaign of anti-Semitism that she first fought mightily from within, including being forced to attend her own party's conference under police protection.

She now wages the fight as a political independent. Who knows what, if anything, will come of the new party she co-founded, Change UK. But in leaving she sent a message that I pray will have powerful echoes: Never bend a knee or sacrifice your dignity.

Never, ever forget to love your neighbor.

An attack on a minority is an attack on you.

This one is simple. When someone is attacked because of her identity and not her ideas, see that as an attack on you. This applies just as much to when Donald Trump said that the Indiana-born Gonzalo Curiel was unfit to serve as a judge because he was a "Mexican" as it does when you hear about a Hasidic man beaten while walking down the street in Crown Heights.

My liberation is bound up with yours—that's a cliché

because it is true. It is the idea behind organizations like HIAS, and it was the motivation behind the Jewish Federation of Greater Pittsburgh's fundraising drive for the victims of the New Zealand mosque attacks, which raised more than $650,000. Alliances that ask you to disavow or distort a fundamental part of yourself are not okay. But alliances that allow you to come as your full self to work for the common good? These are fundamentally Jewish and should be sought out.

Fight, first and foremost, as Americans.

If you are reading this in America, this fight is easier, and not just because anti-Semitism here is not as bad as it is in Europe. It's also because the assertion of American values—hatred of tyrants, love of liberty, freedom of thought and of worship, the notion that all people are created equal—are also the assertion of Jewish ones. And I can't think of ideas more important to fight for than those.

When the anti-Semite attacks Jews, he is also attacking America itself. Not just because there is no greater sign of societal disintegration than the spread of anti-Semitism, but because American and Jewish ideals are harmonious.

I believe in the world-changing propositions and promise of this country. And I believe that the good money is on the bet that it is, still, an exceptional nation. The duty to fight anti-Semitism comes from our duty as

Americans who want this country to survive and thrive and live up to its sacred ideals—ideals that have been put under strain in ways many of us lacked the imagination to anticipate.

The Jewish community—2 percent of this population—cannot go at this problem alone. We have to insist that the societies of which we are a part take a stand against anti-Semites because they are at the core of what erodes the fabric of a civilization.

We have to expose how the far right and the far left are lying about America's story. White supremacists lie by asserting they have American cultural primacy. They do this by erasing the living biblical patrimony that nourished the founders and rings out in the words etched into the bell that rang in 1776 to mark the signing of the Declaration of Independence. Crucially, that monument to freedom was not given the name we now know it by—the Liberty Bell—until the following century when abolitionists adopted it, and its biblical inscription, as an emblem of the universal freedom they were fighting for. And yet those on the far left who insist that Jews are white colonialists in a foreign land are erasing the history of the very place where "proclaim liberty" was first declared.

Those on the far right flirting with the swastika and those on the far left glorifying the hammer and sickle: They are raising the flags of the enemies we defeated. The America that fought those evils is the America that we are fighting for when we fight back against anti-Semitism. If you love this country, if you love freedom and liberalism broadly defined, it is in your interest to eliminate this poison. Don't just do it for the Jews. Do it for yourselves and your families. Do it for this country we all have to share.

Wherever you are, vote for freedom.

Jews thrive in freedom because we represent it by our very existence. The Jewish beliefs that everyone is created in God's image and that it is always wrong to worship false idols have been the bane of empires and dictatorships and slave states for as long as there have been Jews. That is why, as Rabbi Jonathan Sacks has put it, "Jews have always been the irritant of empires because of our insistence on the dignity of the individual and his or her liberty." The more a society prizes freedom, the more Jews thrive.

All of this is instructive when thinking about how we vote. It's a tweak on the kippah question: Does this political party, this movement, this organization, this activist group—whatever—want me to be my most whole self? Or, to be accepted or safe, will I need to hide my true views or cut off parts of who I am? Look for the politicians and the parties and the organizations who want you to be most whole. And support them.

Maintain your liberalism.

I am not convinced that we are living through the 1930s again, but it's clear to me that many people *feel* as if we are—and they are moving politically as a result. Nazis or Communists: You have to choose. Those who were, until recently, on the center right are now turning against liberalism itself. Those once on the center left are doing the same for different reasons. One increasingly worships the state, the other statism.

There is a good reason for this. The center has fallen away, and people do not feel comfortable maintaining political homelessness—which these days means moderation—and so they leap toward ever further extremes, where they are rewarded with a sense of tribal fealty.

None of this is good for a healthy democracy, and none of it is good for the Jews. Worship of the state, which is something we see on the nationalist right, is worship of a false god. And worship of the group over the dignity of the individual, which we are seeing on the far left, is worship of another false deity. History shows us that both end in bloodshed.

Support Israel.

When Jews today in Paris or London or Budapest or San Diego sit around their dinner tables and discuss whether or not they should be packing up, once again, getting out the suitcase that the Jew has carried for thousands of years, we know that our fears and anxieties are fundamentally different from the fears and anxieties of Jews who lived before 1948. We know that, if need be, we could pick up and move tomorrow to a state with an army and nuclear weapons. This sense of security that the existence of Israel provides cannot be overstated. It makes life in an uncertain Brooklyn or Toulouse possible. Anyone who denies this, I believe, is lying to you or to themselves.

Supporting Israel does not mean—I cannot believe I have to say this—never criticizing it. On the contrary, it means demanding that Israel live up to its ideals. But it is also important to hold in tension Israel's flaws with the fact that it is a political and historical miracle. My colleague Roger Cohen put it this way in a recent column: "I don't believe Jews would be just fine without Israel any more than I believe the moon is a balloon. To criticize Israel is imperative; to disavow it, for a Jew, a form of ahistorical folly."

That I can walk the streets of Tel Aviv today as a feminist woman in a tank top, that it is a free and liberated society in the middle of the Middle East, is an achievement so great it is often hard for many people to grasp. We should work hard to appreciate its magnitude.

Maintain the David and Goliath paradox.

Fissures have opened up in the Jewish world: the divide between Americans and Israelis; between the older, more conservative generation and the younger, more liberal one. But I think the most significant division is the one between what I've come to think of as the David people and the Goliath people.

David people think that Jews are always under siege, that another mass murder could be around the corner, that Israel is a tiny outpost in a hostile neighborhood. If David people have a wide-angle lens, Goliath people are zoomed all the way in. They think that the Jews have it really good, that our power greatly outweighs our vulnerability, and that when it comes to the Palestinians, there is no question who has the upper hand. There is truth to both versions. The challenge and the aim is to be able to hold both in tension inside ourselves.

Build community.

Institutions are conservative by nature. In my experience, their consensus seeking has often disappointed. They issue mealy-mouthed press releases, afraid of upsetting one or another constituency, and obsess about steering committees and working papers and process rather than getting things done.

What has not disappointed me—indeed, what has given me the strength to feel like I can fight—is community. My community mirrors the Jewish people: It spans many time zones and states and countries, but has a shared language and set of goals.

Just as almost nothing in Judaism can be done alone—ten people are needed to make a minyan to pray—nothing in life can be done alone. The work of fighting anti-Semitism requires a band of Maccabees. So find yourself that band. If one doesn't already exist, build it.

Do not divide. Multiply.

That's the wise communal arithmetic my friend Liel Leibovitz observed in Pittsburgh in the days following the shooting. As he wrote for *Tablet*:

> Rather than belong to one shul and refuse to set foot in any other, people here take out multiple memberships, going to one house of worship to be with some friends, say, to another to hear a wise rabbi speak, and to a third to enjoy some beautiful liturgy. On Shabbat Teshuvah, the Shabbat between Rosh Hashanah and Yom Kippur, one soft-spoken Orthodox immigrant who settled in Pittsburgh after fleeing the anti-Semitic climate of Paris told us, some synagogues across town unite, nominating one rabbi to address their shared congregations. None of this is to say that important distinctions—theological, political, and emotional—aren't observed or respected; they are. But they are never allowed to grow so ravenous or so wild as to de-

vour the community they ultimately serve, a community that insists on always remaining larger than the sum of its parts.

Amen.

If you find yourself standing alone, know that you are in good company.

Loneliness has been part of being a Jew in the world since, well, the very first Jew of all. Can you imagine a lonelier story than that of Abraham's life?

Here is a man who was called by God to smash the idols his father and his community worshipped, to leave the city where he was raised, and to become a nomad. All based on a promise from God that he would eventually be the father of a great nation. Oh, and along the way he would be called on by that same God to offer up his son Isaac as a sacrifice. It wasn't exactly an easy life.

Abraham's story is deeply Jewish. He stood radically against the prevailing orthodoxy of his time. You don't need to believe the literal truth of the Abraham story to be struck by the ideals it illustrates: the refusal to worship false idols and the courage to be out of step with those around you.

Today, the idols are more abstract than the ceramics Terah, Abraham's father, prayed to. They come in the form of power and prestige. And the temptation to keep your mouth shut about your convictions in order to get ahead, to get along, and to be well liked is very seductive.

When it comes to politics, American Jews today are a lot like our nomadic ancestor. It is incumbent on us in the face of this loneliness to be like Abraham. To be brave enough to say, Yes, we are different. We are part of a tradition that is far bigger than this current political moment—a tradition that will help us through it. We need to be courageous enough to stand apart, not to bend to the crowd, not to give in to groupthink.

We should find strength and pride in being an idol-smashing people.

Knowing when to stand alone depends on knowing exactly what you are fighting for.

Da lifnei mi atah omed. Know before whom you stand. That phrase is inscribed over the ark in many if not most synagogues around the world.

Maybe you stand before God. Perhaps you are one of the lucky people who feel sure of that. As for me, I try to live as if I do. I resonate with the way the late Charles Krauthammer described himself to me: as a Shinto Jew. He was referring to ancestor worship, but of course the Jews already venerate their ancestors, as he surely knew. Three times every day, we pray to the God of Abraham, Isaac and Jacob, Sarah, Rebecca, Rachel and Leah, naming each of them.

I stand before the valor and the sacrifices of my ancestors. I stand before the iconoclasm of Abraham and Sarah. I stand before the faith of Rabbi Akiva and the courage of Hannah Senesh. I stand before the brazenness of the Maccabees, before the compassion of Ruth and the optimism of Anne Frank and the audaciousness of Ben-Gurion.

That is my proud legacy. That is my inheritance. That is the line I want to be part of, however tiny my role. And it is not a line of blood. The biblical Ruth, after all, was a convert from one of the most hated groups of people in the Bible, the Moabites. She left her tribe and followed her mother-in-law, Naomi, back to the land of Israel. It is Ruth's line that Jews believe would give the world King David and, ultimately, the Messiah.

In other words, the line is not genetic; it is a line of choice. Look ahead of you and look behind you. Who are you bringing along to join our everlasting chain?

As Walker Percy once asked,

Why does no one find it remarkable that in most world cities today there are Jews but not one single Hittite, even though the Hittites had a flourishing civilization while the Jews nearby were a weak and obscure people?

When one meets a Jew in New York or New Orleans or Paris or Melbourne, it is remarkable that no one considers the event remarkable. What are they doing here? But it is even more remarkable to wonder, if there are Jews here, why are there not Hittites here? Where are the Hittites? Show me one Hittite in New York City.

I do not know the ultimate reason why great empires have fallen and yet millions of Jews all over the world still recite the Shema in the same language. What I think we can strive for, if not the answer, is to be ever grateful for the miracle.

Lean into Judaism.

In December 1897, Theodor Herzl wrote a short essay called "The Menorah." The essay is in the form of a parable, and the subject is clearly Herzl himself. I also suspect that the subject could be many of you, just as it could have been written today. "Once there was a man who deep in his soul felt the need to be a Jew. His material circumstances were satisfactory enough. He was making an adequate living and was fortunate enough to have a vocation in which he could create according to the impulses of his heart," Herzl begins.

> He had long ceased to trouble his head about his Jewish origin or about the faith of his fathers, when the age-old hatred re-asserted itself under a fashionable slogan. Like many others, our man, too, believed that this movement would soon subside. But instead of getting better, it got worse. Although he was not person-

ally affected by them, the attacks pained him anew each time. Gradually his soul became one bleeding wound.

If you are reading this book, perhaps you identify with something of the above.

The account continues:

This secret psychic torment had the effect of steering him to its source, namely, his Jewishness, with the result that he experienced a change that he might never have in better days because he had become so alienated: He began to love Judaism with great fervor. At first he did not fully acknowledge this mysterious affection, but finally it grew so powerful that his vague feelings crystallized into a clear idea to which he gave voice: The thought that there was only one way out of this Jewish suffering—namely, to return to Judaism.

When his best friends, whose situation was similar to his, found out about this, they shook their heads and thought that he had gone out of his mind. How could something that only meant an intensification and deepening of the malady be a remedy? He, on the other hand, thought that the moral distress of modern Jews was so acute because they had lost the spiritual counterpoise which our strong forefathers had possessed.

What is amazing is how far Herzl had come and in how short a time. In 1893, he had proposed, in print, the mass conversion of Austria's Jews at St. Stephen's Cathedral in Vienna. He ultimately woke up from that despair. Conversion was not the answer. The answer was right there in the Bible. The answer was for the Jews to choose life—whole lives, not partial ones. The answer in our day is just the same.

Yisroel Goldstein exemplified the spirit of our ancestors on the morning of April 27, 2019. Two of his fingers had been shot. He would go on to lose one of them. And yet before he would allow himself to be taken to the hospital, he offered these words of Torah: "In every generation they rise against us to destroy us; and the Holy One, blessed be God, saves us from their hand. Am Yisrael Chai. The people of Israel live."

Nurture your Jewish identity—and that of those around you.

Maybe it's deciding to have Shabbat dinner every week. Maybe it's making the choice to send your children to Jewish day school. Maybe it is booking a trip to Israel, or binge-watching *Shtisel* on Netflix or reading the poetry of Yehuda Amichai or the novels of David Grossman or Geraldine Brooks. Maybe it's signing up for classes on Jewish mysticism or meditation. Maybe it's subscribing to a Jewish or Israeli newspaper, or giving a gift to a charity you admire.

Cultivating and strengthening your Jewish identity may not seem like an obvious way to combat anti-

Semitism, but it is actually one of our most powerful weapons. That is especially the case for parents, who have the opportunity to raise educated, proud, and joyful Jews of the next generation.

This year in Jerusalem, I asked one of my heroes, Natan Sharansky, if it was possible to teach people to be brave. Of all the people I have ever met, he was best in a position to know, having spent nine years in the Soviet gulag for the crime of wanting to emigrate to Israel. When he was in solitary confinement, he would play chess in his head to keep himself from going insane. What did this bravest man have to impart about teaching bravery? "You can't teach anyone to be brave," he told me. "All you can do is show them how good it feels to be free."

Know that one person can change history. Is it you?

If we have learned one thing from history, it is that the ending is never predetermined. If Churchill had not possessed his singular resolve, we might all be speaking German today.

Herzl was an assimilated, wealthy Jew who barely spoke Hebrew. A journalist and playwright, he woke up to his Judaism and his people because of the anti-Semitism he saw in his midst, which pushed him toward a radical solution. In 1896 he wrote a short book making his argument: *Der Judenstaat,* "The Jewish State."

"No one can deny the gravity of the situation of the

Jews. Wherever they live in perceptible numbers, they are more or less persecuted," he wrote. The only recourse was the Jewish return to political sovereignty in their indigenous land after more than two thousand years of exile.

The book concludes: "Therefore I believe that a wondrous generation of Jews will spring into existence. The Maccabees will rise again. Let me repeat once more my opening words: The Jews who wish for a State will have it. We shall live at last as free men on our own soil, and die peacefully in our own homes."

Two years later, in 1897, he did something that many people thought was a joke. He called a Zionist Congress in Basel. He asked the two hundred delegates to wear tails to signify the formality and the seriousness of the occasion.

"This is no longer the elegant Dr. Herzl of Vienna; it is a royal descendant of David arisen from the grave," one of the delegates wrote. Herzl had a similar sense of the meeting's historic importance. "At Basel I founded the Jewish state. If I said this out loud today, I would be greeted by universal laughter. In five years, perhaps, and certainly in fifty years, everyone will perceive it."

So confident was he that before he died, at the age of forty-four, he said: "I wish to be buried in the vault beside my father, and to lie there till the Jewish people shall take my remains to Israel." In 1949, his bones were taken to Jerusalem.

The spiritual founder of the Jewish state was not a

scholar, nor a rabbi, nor a natural leader. He was a Jew who awakened to the call of history, to the call of his people. Whenever I read about Herzl's remarkable life, I think about another unlikely Jew who saved her people: Queen Esther. In the Purim story, the Jewish people's savior is a woman who had reached the highest ranks of Persian society as the assimilated wife of the king.

When the king's evil vizier, Haman, sets out to kill all of the Jews in the kingdom, Esther hesitates to out herself. To appeal to the king on behalf of her people would likely mean her own death. Her uncle Mordechai says to her, "Do not imagine that you, of all the Jews, will escape with your life by being in the king's palace. On the contrary, if you keep silent in this crisis, relief and deliverance will come to the Jews from another quarter, while you and your father's house will perish. And who knows, perhaps you have attained your position for just such a crisis."

Look at your own life. Perhaps you have attained your own royal position for this very moment. The point of the power we've accumulated isn't just to be on the side of people who are in power, which is what we learned in exile. It is to use it.

Tell your story.

The proper—and ultimately the only—response to this moment is to practice a Judaism of affirmation, not a Judaism of defensiveness.

That is what Lori Gilbert-Kaye, who was murdered in Poway, did. If someone was sick and needed a meal, Lori organized it. If they needed a ride to chemo, Lori was there. She would give Easter baskets to kids even though that's not exactly a Jewish tradition. As everyone who knew her has attested, Lori personified *hesed,* loving-kindness. She is the best of the Jewish people, and we should emulate her fine life.

As yet another of my rabbis, Noa Kushner of the Kitchen in San Francisco, said on the Shabbat after Poway: "Only living Torah, only what is happening in this room and of course, many other places, only Shabbat, only this living Torah can be an appropriate response to senseless destruction. Not only because these rituals and ways of life are just that, ways of *life for the living.* But because these commandments help us protect the parts of us *no fence can secure.*"

You see the right way to fight this disease of anti-Semitism by telling our story—the epic story of the history of our people—especially to the younger generation.

What is the probability that the people of Israel driven, as Moses put it, out to the farthest parts under heaven, would, in fact, come back to their ancient land to rejoin the remnant that remained from the corners of the earth, after two thousand years of exile, of persecution, of destruction, of expulsion, and of near elimination? That a people so despised would survive and thrive? These are earthly miracles just as amazing as the parting of the Red Sea.

We should be telling that epic story, especially to the younger generation.

We should not dumb it down. Big ideas changed my life. And nothing has been more powerful in my life than feeling like I am a part of the Jewish story, a tiny link in our history. In these trying times, our best strategy is to build, without shame, a Judaism and a Jewish people and a Jewish state that are not only safe and resilient but self-aware, meaningful, generative, humane, joyful, and life-affirming. A Judaism capable of lighting a fire in every Jewish soul—and in the souls of everyone who throws in their lot with ours.

There are many forces in our world insisting, again, that all Jews must die. But there is a force far, far greater than that. And that is the force of who we are. We are a people descended from slaves who brought the world ideas that changed the course of history. One God. Human dignity. The sanctity of life. Freedom itself.

That is our inheritance. That is our legacy. We are the people commanded to bring light into this world.

Do we believe in our own story? Can we make it real once again? I believe that we can. And that we must.

ACKNOWLEDGMENTS

So many people have shaped my ideas about this subject, but I would be remiss if I did not thank those who had a direct role in this project.

I am proud to be represented by Kathy Robbins. Through her, I was lucky to find a home with Gillian Blake at Crown, who has shepherded through this book with the rare combination of great care and breakneck speed. My thanks to the whole team at Crown, especially Julie Cepler, Dyana Messina, and Caroline Wray. Evan Camfield and Bonnie Thompson had my back. Penny Simon went above and beyond. Thank you, also, to Casiana Ionita, my editor at Penguin Press in the U.K.

Seth Siegel and his team have been tireless in their efforts to get me in front of the right audiences. I am grateful, also, to my friends at the Singer Foundation, the Schusterman Foundation, and the Anti-Defamation

League, particularly Jonathan Greenblatt and David Weinberg.

This book would not have happened without the wisdom and guidance of Jonathan Rosen and the support of his—my second—family. All mistakes in these pages are my own, but I am indebted to Hillel Ofek, Adam Rubenstein, Alex Zeldin, and Sam Zieve-Cohen, who provided expert fact checking and research support. David Samuels's insights were invaluable.

I am grateful to my first newspaper editor, David B. Green at *Ha'aretz,* and to Seth Lipsky, who gave me my first job in journalism at *The New York Sun.* I learned to write and edit at *The Wall Street Journal,* and no one taught me more than Bret Stephens.

I no longer work at *Tablet,* but will forever be proud of my association with the magazine, which managed to anticipate this book's themes by months and sometimes years, and of my friendships with Stephanie Butnick and Liel Leibovitz. *Tablet* is presided over by my dear friend Alana Newhouse, who is one of the great impresarios of the American Jewish community.

There is nothing like *The New York Times,* and I am lucky to work there with Honor Jones, my editor, and James Bennett and Jim Dao, who supported me and this project from the start.

Bill Maher and every person at *Real Time* have been unfailingly generous and kind.

In our collective fight against anti-Semitism, I am

grateful to have connected to Neil Blair, Noam Dworman, Dara Horn, Robbie Kaplan, Alex Levy, Dan Loeb, Meghan McCain, Richard and Lisa Plepler, Lynn Schusterman, Susan Silverman, Dan Shapiro, Natan Sharansky, Matthew Weiner, and Einat Wilf. And to have deepened my friendships with Dan Ahdoot, Meryl Ainsman, Frank Bruni, Daniella Greenbaum Davis, Caitlin Flanagan, David French, Matti Friedman, Josh Glancy, Jeffrey Goldberg, Mark Horowitz and Jennifer Senior, Terry Kassel, Jamie Kirchick, Eli Lake, Bernard Henri-Levy, Gady Levy, Deborah Lipstadt, Andy Mills, Michael Moynihan, Tariro Mzezewa, Michael Oren, Abby Pogrebin, Nancy Rommelmann, Julie Sandorf, Dan Senor, Cindy Shapira, Ruth Wisse, and Brian Zittel.

Every Jew needs a rabbi. I am lucky to have more than my fair share. Thank you especially to Angela Warnick Buchdahl, Jamie Gibson, Daniel Gordis, David Ingber, Noa Kushner, Danny Schiff, Motti Seligson, Mychal Springer, Joseph Telushkin, and David Wolpe. Yossi Klein Halevi, who never went to rabbinical school, has nevertheless been a rebbe to me since college.

I am lucky to have David Busis, Leora Fridman, Avromi Kanal and Sarah Shaw, David Levinson, Leslie Niren, Tina Romero, Evan Hepler-Smith, Ilana Tarr, and Thomas Whittington in my corner. The United States Marine Corps has an unofficial motto, coined by General Jim Mattis: no better friend, no worse enemy. That is how I think about the following people: Ariel Beery, David and Allie Droz, David and Sarah Feith, Rachel Fish, Jordan and Samara Hirsch, Aharon Horowitz, Daniella Kahane, and Ben and Ali Kander.

Above all and always: Jen Spyra and Benjy Shaw.

Nellie Bowles made a California home for me while I wrote this book.

I feel the support of the Weiss-Steiner-Mullen-Kander-Carpenter-McCafferty families of Pittsburgh wherever I go. My beloved sisters, Casey, Molly, and Suzy, are my tribe of tribes.

And finally, to my parents, Amy and Lou Weiss. The greatest honor of my life is being their daughter.

ABOUT THE AUTHOR

BARI WEISS is a staff writer and editor for the Opinion section of *The New York Times*. Weiss was an op-ed and book review editor at *The Wall Street Journal* before joining the *Times* in 2017. She has also worked at *Tablet*, an online magazine of Jewish politics and culture. A native of Pittsburgh, she now lives in New York City.

bariweiss.com
Twitter: @bariweiss

ABOUT THE TYPE

This book was set in Minion, a 1990 Adobe Originals typeface by Robert Slimbach. Minion is inspired by classical, old-style typefaces of the late Renaissance, a period of elegant and beautiful type designs. Created primarily for text setting, Minion combines the aesthetic and functional qualities that make text type highly readable with the versatility of digital technology.